JOYS OF HUNTING ANTIQUES

Illustrations by Hilda Simon

GLOSSARY BY THE AUTHOR

Stefan Salter

JOYS OF HUNTING
ANTIQUES

HART PUBLISHING COMPANY, INC.   NEW YORK CITY

COPYRIGHT © 1971,

HART PUBLISHING COMPANY, INC.

LIBRARY OF CONGRESS

CATALOG CARD NUMBER 71-151632

SBN NUMBER 8055-1092-3

MANUFACTURED IN THE UNITED STATES

DESIGNED BY STEFAN SALTER ASSOCIATES

Drawing on an almost encyclopedic fund of information, the author discusses how certain artifacts were made, emphasizing the distinguishing characteristics which make for quality in certain pieces.

This book will appeal to anyone who loves antiques and would love to spend a few hours in the company of a highly cultured man of great charm.

Perhaps what is most remarkable about this book is not that it was written by a man who, today, is almost totally blind, but that it was *designed* by a man who sees only in his mind's eye. The clarity and incisiveness of his artistic perception will be evident to anyone who turns these pages.

The book is enhanced by more than 80 drawings in full color, rendered by Hilda Simon, an artist of formidable reputation who has illustrated a number of award-winning books.

STEFAN SALTER Always a busy man and always occupied with professional projects, Stefan Salter nevertheless traveled extensively in Europe and in the United States during his vacations, never omitting stops at any likely antique shop he happened to pass. He thinks of himself not as a collector, but as a lover of antiques, and, has surrounded himself in his home in Connecticut with his precious finds.

Stefan Salter is one of the small group of men and women whose artistic background and technical skill have so largely determined the increasingly high standards of American book design in the last 35 years. Educated in England and Germany, Mr. Salter brought to American book publishing devotion to fine craftsmanship and a love of literature. His influence on American book design has been far-reaching; and his work, recognized throughout the world of graphic arts, has won wide acclaim and many awards.

About eight years ago, Mr. Salter lost his sight. However, his apprehension of the printed page is so keen that today he still designs a great number of books for leading publishers.

HILDA SIMON Born in Santa Ana, California, Hilda Simon was taken to Europe by her parents when she was but a child. She remained in Germany about 15 years, where she majored in art and biology—two disciplines that were to become the foundation of her life.

She returned to the United States shortly after World War II, where she continued her studies of natural history, and became a professional artist. Through the years, Miss Simon developed her own method of color illustration: a technique which does not require the usual camera separation. By dint of her own sophisticated process, she achieved the startling color results which have won so much acclaim.

Miss Simon is the author of a number of books; some of these have won awards. Of course, she has illustrated all her texts. A friend of Stefan Salter for many years, Miss Simon readily lent her talents to illustrating this book on antiques. This is her first venture in delineating inanimate objects.

To my wife Mary who helped so much

The Chapters

The Introduction

During the years in which I have hunted for and purchased antiques, I have always seen more than I could use and sometimes at higher prices than I could afford. I rarely acquired antiques because they were cheap. What I wanted, I bought happily and have enjoyed through the years. My antiques owe me nothing. I have not become a collector for the sake of collecting, nor an investor for the sake of making money. The antiques in my home almost look as if the house had been built around them. Many times I hear people say, "You can't touch antiques anymore. The prices are out of reach." That may be so, but I know that with patience and perseverance you can even now find treasures similar to those I have acquired at reasonable prices.

Outlandish prices for antiques are usually demanded by dealers who do not really know the field. Such prices are paid by the gullible who do not take the trouble to learn anything about the treasures they might find.

Most museums—and certainly all folk art museums in Europe and historical societies in America—will acquaint you with the artifacts of our diverse Western cultures. The tremendous wealth of material and the high quality museum pieces should not discourage the prospective collector.

Of the museums which most stimulated my interest in

antiques, I might mention the Philadelphia Museum of Art, the Metropolitan Museum of Art (New York), and the Museum of Fine Arts (Boston).

Two of the great folk art museums of the world are the Landeskunst Museum of Munich and the Landeskunst Museum of Innsbruck. There is also a great collection of antiques of the pre-Baroque period in the Rijksmuseum in Amsterdam. The Victoria and Albert Museum in London houses all that is dear to British culture.

Perhaps the most impressive museum in the world, displaying collections of primitive furniture as well as fine furniture and artifacts, is the DuPont collection in Winterthur, Delaware. Built in the style of their ancestral home and named after Winterthur, Switzerland, from whence the DuPonts came, this family has truly spared no effort to collect and show all that is beautiful in the culture of the colonies and of the early Republic.

Needless to say, I have never been in any town or city without seeking out its museums.

What is it about antiques that fills me with such pleasure when I look at them? Foremost, the enjoyment in seeing creative work. Through the ages men and women have always had the urge to create beautiful objects. I have watched needlework come to life in the hands of my mother. I have seen an Austrian wood carver make the figures which were going to be painted for a crèche at Christmas. I have admired Spanish blacksmiths making the intricate iron scroll work which adorns so many Spanish houses. Wherever I could, I have watched people make things, or have read about them. I have compared old wallpapers and stencils for wall decorations and found them almost identical to colorful papers used in the binding of books. Seeing such things, centuries after they were made, has been exciting.

In writing this book I have made an effort to remember, at least approximately, how much I may have paid for each article. Sometimes my memory yielded the answer, sometimes not, as antique hunting has been one of my activities for the last forty years. In 1931, $90 for an old corner cabinet was a lot of money. In 1945, paying the the same sum would have been considered an excellent buy. And in 1962, you could not buy a corner cabinet for less than $250. Today, $500 or more would be considered a fair price.

Appreciating and understanding dollar values of antiques presupposes familiarity with the economies of the last four decades. In these pages, I have sometimes said that an antique was "modestly priced." Sometimes I have not mentioned any price. My memory tells me that I bought practically everything at a reasonable figure and had to extend my finances only a very few times. Through the years, all my antiques have increased substantially in value.

Sometimes, I regret not having invested a good deal of money buying up many antiques, mostly because the opportunity to buy those particular things would hardly come again. Since it has never been my intention to maintain a personal museum or to become a commercial dealer, I bought only what I really wanted and, more importantly, what I could really use.

Usually I was patient, and bought only when the price was right. But I was always confident that something would "turn up presently," as Mr. Micawber of *David Copperfield* would say.

I am grateful to Mrs. Rachel Baker for her many good suggestions in the final preparation of the manuscript, and especially to Mrs. G. Brett Hollerith and to my wife who helped to assemble my material.

I have tried to recount faithfully what my adventures in antique hunting have been. The antiques in my home are silent witnesses. They come to life in these pages through the art of Hilda Simon.

Old Greenwich, Connecticut
Spring 1971

JOYS OF HUNTING ANTIQUES

Uncle Sandor and Aunt Etel

BUDAPEST 1931

The last time I saw my Uncle Sandor was in 1931. A few days later I would be returning to America. Uncle Sandor took me into his workshop and placed a bottle of Tokay and two glasses on the workbench. He filled them both, urged me to drink up, and then started to tell me stories about our families, interspersed with a good bit of heart-felt advice.

When the bottle was empty, he stood up and handed me a tool I had admired for a long time. It was a slim carpenter's plane which had once belonged to his grandfather. Surely it was at least one hundred years old. Although my uncle had become a dentist, he loved cabinet-making.

"Don't forget that you have a trade now," he said, jokingly, "a good trade. Don't be ashamed of it, and don't forget your uncle and your aunt."

Uncle Sandor and Aunt Etel were childless. When I was a boy, they often invited me to spend part of my vacation with them. My mother had come from Budapest, and my uncle still lived in the pleasant, hilly suburb of Hüvös Völgy on the other side of the Danube. My aunt, my mother's younger sister, looked very much like my mother. Aunt Etel was sweet, and she spoiled me.

My uncle, a short, stocky man with a walrus moustache and a full, silk tie, had a great sense of humor—but that didn't interfere with his being strict with me. He felt that I should become as fine a cabinetmaker as his grandfather. Presumably, he thought that I would succeed.

When I had the bad fortune of being his dental patient, he would lean over close to my face, breathe heavily, and his moustache would tickle me. His drill was run by a foot treadle. When Uncle Sandor became excited by what he saw in my mouth, he would make the treadle go faster; but whether the drill turned slow or fast, it was very pain-

ful. In those days dentists did not like to give novocaine to their patients. I suffered accordingly.

I said goodbye to Uncle Sandor and to Aunt Etel; and then I walked back to my parents' home.

On the way, I noticed a curio shop with the sign *Antik Regi*. In the window there was a pretty plate with a floral design and the name, Etel, inscribed on it. I was intrigued by the coincidence. I thought of the many times that Aunt Etel had placed a plate with cookies or fruit at my bedside, had let me win at cards, had kissed me as my mother did.

I had never bought an antique before so I asked, hesitatingly, how much the plate cost. It was not expensive, so I timidly bought it.

While the plate was being wrapped, I saw something I thought would please my uncle—a small, collapsible inch measure made of ivory. What was curious was that one side was marked, "Vienna," and the other side, "London." I gathered that the standards of measure had been different in various countries when that little ruler had been made.

The plate and measure were charming. Although I was young, I had learned from my parents to be gracious; and I felt grateful towards both my strict uncle and my indulgent aunt. When I arrived at my parents' home, I left the package with them to give to my uncle and aunt when they would see them again.

A few years later, my father died. Things looked black in Europe—war was imminent. My mother and sister came to America. Soon after she arrived, my mother gave me a little package entrusted to her by Uncle Sandor and Aunt Etel. She said, with tears in her eyes, "I know I'll never see them again." The package contained the plate, the ivory measure and a note which said, "Stay well, dear boy. Now that you will have a home of your own—and maybe a workshop—we want you to have the plate and the ruler to remember us by. Uncle Sandor and Aunt Etel."

Elli and Anni Glaser, Munich, Germany

WHITE PLAINS AND WIESBADEN 1932

November, 1931. It was late afternoon. There was snow on the ground; the air was cold and crisp. I hurried from the darkening parking lot into the Westchester County Center to see the annual antiques show. The warm air inside was welcome, and the many voices sounded like ocean waves in the distance. Down the stairs I went into the vast auditorium. And what a sight it was! Pewter and brass, copper and glass, ceramics, furniture, antique jewelry—there was so much of it, it made me gasp!

Hundreds of dealers had come from all over—from upstate New York, from Pennsylvania, from Virginia and Maryland, from New England, California, and even from Europe.

I, too, had come from Europe—from Germany where the darkness was beginning to fall. Who knew then that there would be years of bitter struggle and suffering for millions.

How irresistibly I was drawn to every exhibit. In those days, I did not know much about antiques, although the home of my parents contained a few noteworthy pieces. But the more I saw at this exhibition, the more I wanted to see.

I stopped in front of a smaller booth, not as crowded as the others. Inside, behind a table covered with antique jewelry, there sat two attractive young women. Not more than two feet behind them hung a large sign lettered much in the same manner as all the others in the show. It read, "Elli and Anni Glaser, Munich." After that, in very small letters was printed "Germany."

When I entered their booth, looking at the merchandise, both ladies deferentially rose. I inspected a piece, here and there. After a while, I found a charming little green wine bottle, one of those used in old inns to measure out a pint of *open wine*. I picked it up and inquired how much it cost.

"Oh, fourteen marks fifty," answer the smaller of the two women, inclining her head eagerly.

"Ach, nein! Elli!" interrupted the other woman, as she shook her head. "It is not in marks, it is in dollars, but how much?" She looked at me and laughed. "*Bitte*, how much is fourteen marks fifty?"

"*Ungefähr* $3.50," I replied.

At once both exclaimed, "How wonderful! You speak German!"

I stayed in their booth the whole evening. Whenever there were no other customers, we talked about antiques, about Munich, and about Berlin, which was my home town. But mostly we talked about the two women themselves, about their home, their family, their life.

Elli was small, a brunette with a very fine, sad face. Her hands were long and elegant. She wore a charming knitted dress. Anni, her half-sister, was tall, and had curly blonde hair. She was sporty in appearance and might easily have been taken for a British lady.

They were fascinating, these two, both lovable and great fun to be with. In the midst of the noise and con-

11

fusion of the exhibition, we became good friends. When closing time came, they wrapped up my purchases which included the wine bottle, a Siamese toy elephant painted gaily in white, red, green and yellow, and a hardwood mortar and pestle. The last-named cost me five dollars, and have often been put to use in my kitchen. Every now and

12

then, I give the two pieces a little coating of oil to revive their warm lustre.

The toy elephant was more expensive, but irresistible. I had also wanted to buy a large tassel made of red, green, and gold cords, but it was priced at more than I could afford in those days, so I reluctantly had to forego it.

During their short stay, the Glaser sisters and I spent as much time together as possible. We had become friends. For life, I thought. When we finally said goodbye, we all cried a little. Before they left, they urged a little package on me. When I opened it at home, it turned out to be the tassel.

When Hitler took over Germany, I began to worry about the safety of my friends. They were both Jewish, although Anni had an Aryan mother, and was married to a man who was only one-quarter Jewish. However, during

the coming years the finer points of arithmetic were to be submerged in a brutal ideology. I rarely heard from them. They hinted they might manage better in Wiesbaden, not being known in that town. And their last letter to me came from there.

Goodbye to Elli and Anni. Goodbye to true aristocracy, and to a fine friendship which had, indeed, lasted a lifetime.

*   *   *

The first time I visited Wiesbaden after the war, I was happy to see that this city had not suffered as much as Frankfurt. It had not been considered a strategic target.

Wiesbaden had become headquarters for the Army of Occupation. Other U.S. offices began to spring up, and it had not taken too much time to restore the particular mixture of easy comfort and spa elegance for which the town had been famous for centuries.

As everywhere, I searched for and found antique shops. But the one I was looking for was situated in a narrow, steep lane. I climbed slowly, and when I found the shop, I was not disappointed. The sign very clearly said, "Antiquitäten." Underneath, in smaller script, it read, "Formerly Elli and Anni Glaser."

I entered the shop and looked around. There was only an elderly lady, dressed conservatively but with elegance, taking care of a customer. She observed me, nodded a friendly greeting, and I felt welcome to browse.

After the other had left, I walked over and asked the price of a beautiful baroque silver ladle. The old lady proceeded to look it up in a book, a practice I do not like as it gives a shopkeeper an opportunity to quote an inflated price after estimating what the customer might be induced to pay.

14

"You have a lot of icons," I said. The statement was half a question and she answered it vaguely, saying, "Oh well, so many things were brought in during the last years . . . there must have been quite a few Russians here."

I pondered this. Perhaps she was referring to slave laborers, perhaps to prisoners, or perhaps to some of the more cultivated soldiers who had unloaded their loot. There was an uncomfortable pause. I could see that she did not view me with affection. I had not wanted to, but I couldn't help it, so I blurted out, "And what happened to the Misses Glaser?"

She was composed enough when she answered. "Oh, I guess they moved away. The store was sold to me by the administration."

I did not ask further. The old lady's lips were tight. In the defensive manner of a person who feels attacked, she looked at me with an unfriendly stare.

It was not difficult to guess where the Misses Glaser had moved. "Grüss Gott!" I said, sadly, and closed the door behind me.

Mrs. Clulow and Miss Patch

CAPE COD 1942

Cape Cod and antique shops are almost synonymous—at least they were in the forties when my wife and I went there to do some antique hunting. I remember some of the shops we visited and some of the dealers, but I particularly remember the gentle widow Clulow and the brisk Miss Patch.

During World War II, gasoline was rationed. We leisurely bicycled around the Cape, rarely seeing a car. So it came about that since we were pedalling along at eight miles an hour, no antique shop on the main roads escaped our attention. There were very few tourists, and the shops were filled with antiques.

In East Falmouth we visited the Red Barn. I remember the owner well. In her gentle way, Mrs. Clulow was a true lady, and we made friends with her easily.

"I wish I had listened to my husband," she said. "He wanted to teach me so much about antiques, but I paid no heed."

Yes, it was true. Mrs. Clulow didn't know too much about antiques, and we were able to tell her a few things for which she was grateful. She was so kind and generous that we had to stop her from giving us things.

Antiques were not expensive then. But we had little money and couldn't buy very much. We tried to concentrate on a few things, but that was quite difficult because we liked everything.

We were particularly fond of glass bottles, partly for the

beauty of their colors and partly because of the interesting shapes that were turned out in the 19th century. We picked up bottle after bottle in turn from Mrs. Clulow's tables. There were whiskey bottles in characteristic cornucopia designs. Some bore historical inscriptions such as "Geo. Washington, Father of Our Country," or "Success to the Railroad," and the like. These whiskey bottles come in many beautiful colors: amber, cobalt blue, and nut brown.

The gin bottles were square, shaped somewhat like milk cartons, the bases smaller than the tops. These bottles are usually dark olive green.

Then there were slender tonic bottles, still more colorful, and we found these immensely appealing. We bought three: one in cobalt, one in aquamarine, and one in purple.

There were also bottles in the shape of violins, and bottles molded like log cabins. Some had contained syrups; some, medicines; and some, snuff. There were also some small, pyramid-shaped ink bottles made in the same colors as the whiskey bottles.

Mrs. Clulow also had a few rare "end of day" bottles, so called because they were made by glass workers at the end of their working day for their wives or sweethearts. Such bottles, made of emerald, cobalt, or clear glass, were cut in interesting shapes. Some had been supplied with a hinged, silver top. These served as perfume containers. We bought two of them.

We saw glass canes and Christmas balls in gold, silver, green, and light blue. Each of these hand-blown balls weighs more than two full boxes of modern, paper-thin Christmas balls.

Nearly every traditional home in New England has a

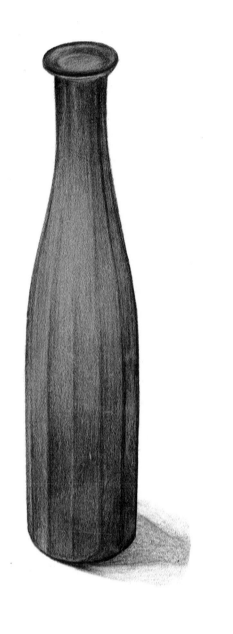
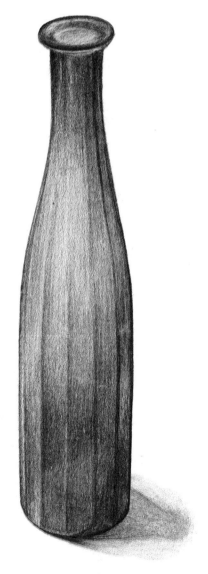

display of colorful bottles somewhere against a window or at the sides of the main door. The sun, playing on these colors, tints the furniture, the floor, and the ever-present doilies, and lends a special charm to these homes.

Mrs. Clulow had invited us into her home, where it became evident that Mr. Clulow had known a good deal about antiques. When we left, we were happy to have made a friend, and pleased to have seen as large and colorful a shop as the Red Barn. Before we departed, we had added to our purchases four fluted, pressed-glass tumblers and an eye-shaped butter mold. With all our bottles, everything came to $18.

We visited many stores that summer in Chatham, Orleans, and Sandwich. In Sandwich we stopped overnight in a house marked "Tourists." For $2 we were put up in an attractive room with a four-poster bed. We ate breakfast with the proprietress, Miss Patch; and, quite naturally, she had an antique shop, too. She carried many lacy Sand-

wich dishes, and we fell in love with a sunburst design. Sandwich mold glass is heavy, always has rough edges, and has a melodic ring. The term *lacy* comes from the brilliancy of this glass. Most Sandwich glass has found its way to private collections and museums. We bought six or seven "honey dishes" and an old pewter saltshaker, all for $15.00.

Some years later, I went to see a very comprehensive exhibit of lacy Sandwich glass at Lord and Taylor's in New York City. The entire collection, from honey dishes to decorated bowls, was for sale. The store set up an interesting system to dispose of this merchandise. What was not sold during the first week was reduced by ten percent for sale during the second week. Another ten percent was taken off during the third week. One had to take one's chances. As I remember, the sale went on for five weeks. The only trouble was that by the time the price was sufficiently reduced for something I wanted, someone else had beaten me to it. In contrast, in the little shop in Sandwich—hardly as elegant as Lord and Taylor's—we were the only customers, and we had first choice.

Miss Patch of Sandwich was not a gentle widow like Mrs. Clulow, but a brisk maiden lady who tolerated us because there were so few tourists in those days. However, she taught us a number of things about pewter; and in all, it was an interesting experience. Happy with our purchases, we celebrated by buying a large lobster; and Miss Patch made a fine supper for the three of us.

"The Old Dear!

Didn't Know She Was Rentin' Rooms."

WILLIAMSBURG, VIRGINIA 1942

On the way to Virginia Beach to visit a young friend of ours who was in the Navy, we had stopped at Williamsburg. During that day, we had seen much of the interesting restoration, including the Governor's Mansion, and we also had visited some shops. Now it was time to find a room for the night, for the main hostelry, the Lodge, was crowded with officers and their families; and back in 1942 there were no motels as yet in Williamsburg. It was exactly six months after Pearl Harbor.

There was something about a certain beautiful colonial house at the corner of the main street that made us feel that we might find a room there, even though we did not see a tourist sign. We rang the bell. After a while, a little old lady opened the door. She was ancient; her skull shone through her transparent skin like ivory. There was a hint of a melancholy smile on her lips, and her voice was very weak. She looked at us, questioningly, and said, "Yes?"

I would have taken my hat off, but I wasn't wearing one, so I answered in as low and delicate a voice as I could manage, "We are looking for a place to stay tonight, and we haven't been able to find anything as yet."

She looked at us for a moment, then stepped back and motioned for us to follow. We went through a long corridor. She opened a door, put on the light, and pointing to a lovely bedroom with a four-poster and canopy, asked again in a nearly inaudible voice, "Will this do?"

We were very happy to find such a room—far more attractive than any hotel room we had ever been in at any time anywhere, and we said so. After we brought our bags in and had washed up, we planned to go out for dinner, but first spent some time with our hostess in her living room.

She was happy to talk with us. She told us how she had lived in that house all her life, and how Yankee soldiers had been quartered in those very rooms during the "War between the States."

"One was a Lieutenant," she said, her eyes lighting up, "and he was very handsome. His monogram is on this window." She pointed to a windowpane, faintly purple

27

Herr

hōre meine worte
mercke auf meine rede·
Vernimm mein ſchreyen,
mein kōnig und mein Gott; dann ich will vor dir
bätten. Herr frühe wolleſt du meine ſtimme
hōren, frühe will ich mich zu dir ſchicken und
darauf mercken. Pſalm 5.

28

with age. Scratched in the glass were the initials "J. McA." Under it in a childish scrawl was written "M.T." She looked wistfully at the window. "That's me," she said. "It stands for Mary Trevor. I was only thirteen years old then."

The next morning Miss Trevor—for Miss Trevor she still was—told us about an antique shop which belonged to a friend of hers. "Annie," she said, "is only seventy-five years old, but she is most informed."

We found Annie's shop easily enough; and when we told her that Miss Trevor had sent us, she could not have been kinder. "Mary's such a dear old lady," she said. She was happy to show us her treasures. We were particularly taken with an embossed, old English brass bellows which, although quite handsome on our hearth, has not been very helpful in tending a fire.

Like most antique dealers, she was attached to some things which she just hated to sell; but when she saw how keen we were about a cobalt blue, three-mold bottle, she was happy to let us have it.

Perhaps the piece we liked best was a framed Psalm written by hand in German and decorated in the Pennsylvania Dutch manner. According to Annie's story, the piece was probably a sample done by an applicant for the job of teacher in a little country school.

It was war time, and since tourists were scarce, dealers charged very little. The bellows, the Psalm and the bottle made a neat package which we could easily carry and for which we quite happily paid $22.

"Give my regards to Mary," said Annie. "The old dear! Didn't know she was rentin' rooms."

It hadn't occurred to us until then that we had been welcomed into the private home of a gentle stranger.

If You Want Antiques,

Go to Pennsylvania

PENNSYLVANIA 1943

"If you want antiques, go to Pennsylvania," our friends advised us. With no further information and with little money to spend, we set out. We left New York on a Saturday morning, taking the train to Philadelphia. There were few thruways in those days. We didn't own a car; and even if we had, there would have been little gas, for those were the early years of the War.

We arrived at the old Broad Street station quite early. Reasoning that most antique shops would not yet be open, we decided to visit the Philadelphia Museum of Art, thinking that some antiques might be displayed there along with the art treasures.

When we asked an attendant in the nearly empty museum if there were any antiques on display, he waved his hand slightly and said condescendingly, "You'll find some Pennsylvania-Dutch antiques in 4F and 4G."

We hurried through the labyrinthine ways until we found ourselves in what appeared to us to be nothing less than heaven. There were tables and chairs, wardrobes, household articles, and kitchen implements, most of them painted in the rich colors so characteristic of Swiss, German, and Scandinavian folk art. But these pieces were all Pennsylvania-Dutch—a magnificent collection. There were the brightly painted boxes—some with locks but most without—each with a simple wooden hinge which was part of the box top. Such is the ingenuity of poverty, for hardware, in those days, was not for the poor. The bright colors of the home-made paint covered inexpensive wood.

There was also a vast selection of pottery made of the red clay so common in Pennsylvania. All the pottery was decorated, some in white, some in green, and some in green and white. There were pie plates, deep dishes for dumplings, assorted bowls of different sizes and molds. Pennsylvania-Dutch pottery is glazed with a transparent glaze, and then fired.

Sgraffito is a technique used often by the Pennsylvania-Dutch. Here the pottery is first painted with a contrasting glaze; then the design is scratched through to the red clay beneath; then the piece is fired. Usually, additional decorations are added in other colors after the first firing, and then the dish is fired once again.

Practically all the articles we saw had German or Pennsylvania-German names, such as *pieschissel* which means a deep dish for pie (more properly, *Schüssel*). The decorations on these pieces run from simple wavy lines to floral designs, tulips being the favorites. Tulips, of course, evidence the Dutch influence. However, tulip designs are equally popular with the Swedes and the Swiss. Some of the loveliest plates in the Museum were decorated in a most intricate manner in several colors. Many of these were adorned with inscriptions, usually in High German, written in *Fraktur*, a broken lettering commonly used by Germans, Dutch, Swiss, and Scandinavians until the early part of the 20th century. All Pennsylvania-Dutch lettering and printing is referred to as Fraktur.

In the museum, baptismal certificates—*Taufscheine*—hung on the walls. These were abundantly illustrated with an

Geburts= und Taufschein.

Diesen beyden Ehegatten,

Als: _Anton Gaul_ und seiner ehelichen Haus-
frau _Magdalena_ eine gebohrne _Fritz_
ist ein _Sohn_ zur Welt gebohren, den 11ten Tag _Merz_
im Jahr unsers HErrn 1822 Dieser _Sohn_ ist gebob-
ren in _Schüllkill, F._ in _Berks_ County, im Staat
Pennsilvanien in Nord=Amerika, und ist getauft worden und er-
hielt den Namen _Amos_ den 7ten Tag
April im Jahr unsers HErrn 1822 von Hrn. _Schäfer_
Die Taufzeugen waren _Daniel Gaul und seine_
Frau Elisabetha.

Reading,
Gedrukt und zu haben bey
Heinrich B. Sage.

array of flowers, birds, angels, as well as the hex signs often seen on Pennsylvania-Dutch barns.

After we had seen our fill, we became eager to get going with our antique hunting. We asked a friendly person at the information desk where we might find antique shops. She showed us a road map and indicated Allentown and Kutztown and New Hope. She was very patient and directed us to a bus which would take us to the Delaware River and New Hope.

We got into an old bus and bounced along to that pleasant, small town. Once there, we lost no time in looking for antique shops. There were two or three on the main street; but a brief inspection did not reveal much of interest, and it was soon time for lunch. We located a small restaurant offering home-cooked food. What good fortune to find that our waitress knew just the places to look for antiques! They were located in the countryside, but taxi fares were much lower then.

Our first stop was a beautiful mansion surrounded by flower gardens. It was positively a dream house. A small handsomely-lettered sign near the door announced simply "Antiques." When we entered the spacious front parlor, the owner of the shop, an attractive middle-aged woman, greeted us coolly. I imagine we looked a little rumpled. Antique shop owners cannot always tell who will buy and who will not; and it is true that there is an unending stream of visitors to such shops who come merely to browse and who buy very little. A shopkeeper's apparent indifference is quite understandable.

What we saw was in good taste and well displayed. We bought two New Jersey pie plates made of yellow clay. The borders indented just like a pie crust that has been cut off with a crimper. The pie plates had never been used, and somehow this has prevented us from using them in the oven all these years. There is something special about an antique that has been preserved completely in its original condition, perhaps because one rarely finds such an article.

Then we saw a set of eight matched goblets in a deep aquamarine *Baccarat* crystal. I picked up one of the glasses. On the bottom there was a label which read, "Set of 8, $4.00." The glasses were magnificent in their brilliance. I turned to the proprietress to inquire the price of the set. Her answer, "$32," told us it was time to go.

We returned to our waiting taxi to continue our search. Finally, as the sun was setting, we came to a weather-beaten sign which read, "M. Yoder, Furniture, Old and New."

When we walked into the house, we saw no one. After a little while, a plain-looking man appeared. Obviously, he was Mr. Yoder. He greeted us, and followed us as we began to inspect the rooms of his house which were lined from floor to ceiling with shelves, each room crammed with wooden implements, glassware, pottery, pewter, brass, or copper.

Who hasn't read in his childhood about caves or rooms in palaces filled with silver and gold, pearls and rubies? Who has not dreamed of finding a treasure of paintings, or a treasure of historical documents, or a treasure of precious stones. This was it—admittedly in a minor key—but most certainly a treasure of antiques.

Everything was stacked neatly. I am sure that there must have been *thousands* of different things. It would have taken a long time to examine them all!

We bought a cherry-wood rolling pin carved with deep grooves for cutting out noodles. Mr. Yoder, who until then had been quite taciturn, now cheered up and placed the rolling pin in a large wooden basket which he obviously expected us to fill. It was a little like going through a grocery shop, picking up item after item.

In every room there was something we wanted. We bought a brass powder horn embossed on both sides with the American Eagle, complete with arrows and branch.

Next we found a brass candle holder and a deep Pennsylvania pieschissel decorated and glazed in two colors. A veteran of both fireplace and oven, it was black at the bottom, and when we got home it bravely resisted our attempts to clean it. However, we found it entirely sturdy and practical. We continue to use it to this day. We bought smaller pie plates made of the same material.

On the upper floor, we couldn't resist a mallard decoy. We also happily came upon two Pennsylvania-Dutch taufscheine, both printed in Reading. They were decorated with angels, birds, and German proverbs. One taufschein, colored charmingly by hand, recorded the birth of a son to a couple who had resided in "Schulkill Kaunty."

Mr. Yoder had quietly filled two baskets. When he hopefully picked up a third, I made a quick approximation of how much we might owe. It was surprisingly little, but so was my salary in those days. I stopped him.

Outside, the darkness had quietly fallen. We hadn't given a thought to where we might stay, or for that matter, have dinner. Mr. Yoder solved the problem for us by inviting us to stay with him. We wondered, silently, where he could put us up. We had seen a room with bedsteads and with quilts, but he motioned us to his pick-up truck. We rattled over uneven country roads to a cheerful little house, where in the kitchen with the family, we were fed dinner at a $1.00 apiece.

We sat at an oilcloth-covered table and tried to fit in with the friendly country folk. Mrs. Yoder ladled out soup with liver dumplings. As the soup plates were large, the soup was, in itself, a meal. But pot roast followed, surrounded by boiled potatoes and red cabbage. In conclusion, Mrs.

Yoder set on the table two big apple pies, still steaming hot. Everybody drank up large mugs of coffee—even the children.

After the meal, we retired to the parlor; and what a parlor it was! It was obvious that Mr. Yoder knew a good deal about antiques, certainly more than we did; and he agreed to tell us how he had come to find them.

"During the first terrible years of the Depression," he said, "I had to do something to keep the family from starving. These antique fellers came from New York and Philadelphia, and they made a deal with me to drive around to the farmers and buy up what I could in old furniture. They paid me so much a load, and if I hustled enough I could fill a truck every day. Then they came in their station wagons and took the better pieces. Some of the other stuff was left with me; and after a while, I learned the business. In a couple of years, I knew enough to pick a few of the best things for myself, and that's what you see in this room."

"And the house?" I inquired. "Your shop? When did you get that?"

"Oh that," he said, lightly. "It was on a little farm I bought, and I used it as a storehouse until I went into business for myself."

Mrs. Yoder nudged her husband with her elbow. "Tell the folks about your other business," she said, beaming proudly. Mr. Yoder informed us that he was in the real estate business, and was also part owner of a bowling alley.

For $2 we spent the night comfortably in one of the Yoders' guest rooms. After a most hearty breakfast which cost us 50¢ each, Mr. Yoder drove us to a bus stop, gratis. I said, "*Auf Wiedersehn!*" But we never did get a chance to return.

Boston By the River and By the Station

BOSTON 1944

I had planned to see Bunker Hill and Faneuil Hall and to spend the afternoon at the Fine Arts Museum in Boston, but my wife had other plans. She wanted to see antique shops.

It was a lovely summer day. We walked slowly down Beacon Hill where we had been staying in an old-fashioned hotel. We admired the comfortable-looking brick houses with their tall windows and green shutters, homes of the old Boston families. The windows, reaching from floor to ceiling, contained many square panes which showed the delicate amethyst color peculiar to some glass which has been exposed to the sun for many years.

Past the Commons, down on Charles Street next to the Charles River, we found many fine old antique shops. One could see at a glance that they were elegant and reserved.

We went into the first shop. There were no prices on the articles. The salesman looked more like a banker than a shopkeeper. We might have bought something to show that we were not "just looking," but when we asked the price of a certain paperweight and then after being told, put it back on the table, the dealer said frostily, "Perhaps these are not exactly what you are looking for. I suggest you try Atlantic Street near the North Station."

We followed his advice; but when we looked at the shops

on Atlantic Street, we found those to be nothing better than thrift shops and junk shops. We realized that we had been the victims of a cruel lesson; and we decided, then

45

and there, to be less timid. We went back to Charles Street where we went from shop to shop.

Systematically, we took a mental inventory of what was offered in each store. Where prices were not marked, we asked for them without embarrassment. Then we took time out for lunch. We would pretend that we were seasoned dealers, or perhaps agents acting for a stingy millionaire. We set ourselves a quota of $50.

Finally, we found a shop in which we bought a few but choice antiques. Among them were four old wine glasses for less than $15—glasses not as fine as the traditional well-decorated Rhine wine glasses, but nevertheless comfortable to hold, and because of their deep emerald hue, suitable for white as well as red wine. We paid for the four plus a glass pitcher of similar color.

A toy wooden horse attracted our attention, and holding it we wondered what had become of the child who had played with it sixty years ago.

Then we saw a small cottage chest marked at $35, and we had to conceal our excitement. Immediately we knew what we were told many times in later years, that it was a very unusual piece, if only because of its small size. Unlike many chests of drawers of the early 19th century, the sides of this piece were solid. Though the chest did not have the light elegance of Chippendale, it had obviously been made by a master craftsman.

We were told that ordinarily a purchaser would have to pay for crating and shipping; but in view of our having bought the glasses and the pitcher, an allowance would be made for crating. Besides, the owner honestly admitted that the hardware now on the chest was not old. Recognizing original metal handles is not easy. Beware of the dealer who tells you that all the hardware on his furniture is old.

When we left the store, we had paid $53.75. Eventually, the cottage chest arrived—express collect! By that time, we had been looking forward to its arrival so eagerly we didn't mind the additional charge.

Mr. Edwin Spooner,

Gentleman Antique Dealer

MAINE 1947

In the summer of 1938, I spent two happy weeks in a farm-house in Maine. It seems unbelievable now, but the cost of room and board was $2 a day. Before I had come to this rather remote area, I had heard much about the antique shops and low prices in the vicinity of the lakes near Bridgeton. At the time, I needed furniture; and prices for antiques were lower than prices of new furniture purchased in stores.

Someone had suggested that Bridgeton and Venice would make good hunting grounds. So there I went by bus to spend the last two days of my vacation. And in North Bridgeton I found what I was looking for—the perfect New England antique shop.

As I walked through the door of Mr. Spooner's white clapboard house, a few little bells announced my arrival. Mr. Spooner, a slender old gentleman, made me feel at home. The better part of his house was decorated in the finest colonial style. It was hard to say whether the shop was a home, or the home, a shop. There was no clutter, though there was an abundance of material. Prices were clearly marked on small cards. I have rarely seen a finer shop. It was the sort of experience you wish would never come to an end, and that you knew would never be re-peated. His place was like a small, wonderful museum.

I felt privileged to be able to buy from him a maple colonial desk and also an unusual sampler, made by a twelve-year-old girl, which listed the first eight Presidents of the United States by their full names.

The desk had a characteristic apron at the bottom, and several drawers under its slanted top. The pigeonholes were delicately fashioned; but to my disappointment I could not find either a false bottom or a secret door. The wood was a fine grade of flaming maple. In old furniture, you can feel the grain of this particular wood. The drawers and sides of this desk were neatly dove-tailed—a true masterpiece of cabinetmaking. The desk cost $90, just what it was marked.

I also bought a pewter porringer of great charm. American pewter is more valuable than pewter from other countries because fewer pieces have survived the rigors of early colonial days.

The porringer was $12—in those days, half of my week's salary.

The sampler cost me less than the curly maple frame which I later ordered in a frame shop.

Up to that point, my visit had been most enjoyable, but I was not prepared for what was to follow. While I was paying for my purchases and Mr. Spooner was wrapping the porringer and sampler, he hesitated for a moment, and then said, "I have something that you might be interested in." He took me into his office. The wall was covered with Currier and Ives prints and maps. Mr. Spooner pointed to a large map and said with a smile, "I could use the space on the wall, and I think you might like this early map of the United States, because it was printed in Europe."

I have always loved maps, and I had even enjoyed drawing them for school assignments. Of course, I loved this map which was printed in France, but part of whose description was written in German. The abbreviations for the States were quaint—sometimes amusing—but the accuracy of the map was beyond question.

I was grateful to Mr. Spooner, for I sensed that he didn't feel it necessary as a business matter to sell the map, and that his offer was a favor to me. I have often found that a common interest between dealer and customer frequently results in a friendly relationship, which is part of the enjoyment of hunting for and collecting antiques.

Sixteen summers later, I stayed in Camden, Maine, for a few weeks. It was uncomfortably hot in the hotel. The beach brought no relief because the waters of Penobscott Bay were icy. So I looked for antique shops. The only one I found in Camden held nothing of interest to me. Sometimes one hunts for pewter and finds furniture; sometimes the reverse is true.

I began to look forward to returning to the air-conditioned comfort of the eight-hour working day in New York City when chance helped me find something I had

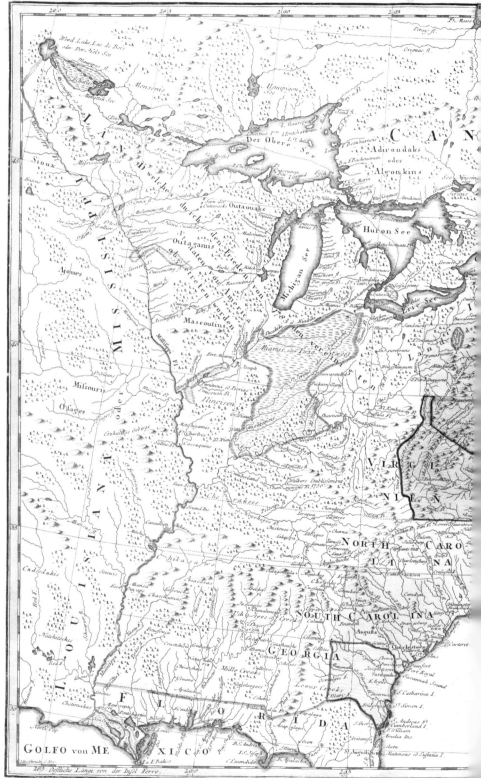

NEU SCHOTTLAND oder ACADIEN

NEU SCHOTTLAND

PROVINZ QUEBEK

PROVINZ QUEBEK

ATLANTISCHES MEER

St. Laurenz Flus

Golfo von St. Laurenz

New Foundland

Long Island

Rhode I.

Boston

NH

NY

M

R

C

NJ

In Staten Island
1. Richmond
In New Jersey.
2. Newark
3. Elizabethtown
4. Morristown
In Pensilvanien.
5. Germantown
6. Bristel
7. Chester
8. Milletown
9. Ephrata
10. Manheim
11. Gimmelstown

CHARTE
über die XIII vereinigte
Staaten von
NORD-AMERICA,
Entworfen durch F. L. Güssefeld,
und herausgegeben von den
Homännischen Erben.

Mit Römisch.Kaiserl.Allergn.
Freyheit. A°. 1784.

Erläuterung der grossen Buchstaben.

M. Provinz Massachusets Bay. NH. New Hampshire.
R. Rhode-Island. C. Connecticut. NY. New York.
NJ. New Jersey. PNS. Pensylvanien. DW. Delaware.
MRL. Mary-land. Die übrigen vier Provinzen sind auf der Charte beschrieben.

Geographische Meilen 15. auf 1. Grad.

See-Meilen 20. auf einen Grad.

Englandische Meilen 69 ½ auf einen Grad.

long been hunting for. The small shop, a few miles north on Penobscott Bay, was located in a house built adjoining a large, well-tended lawn. At the entrance to the shop, there stood a beautiful Sicilian cart with large wheels, the kind still used in Sicily. Decorated in gay colors, the cart was in perfect condition. For a moment I wished I could transfer this lovely vehicle to my own garden. Of course, I realized it would be a major problem to house the cart during the winter, except possibly in my garage which was now filled with bicycles, lawn mowers, and diverse gardening tools. But I walked into the charming house, and inside I found my coffeepot—something I had been searching for, for a long time.

It was a pewter coffeepot, very much in the shape of Georgian silver. The American colonists could not afford silver. Pewterers copied the styles used by the British aristocracy in everything from candleholders to coffeepots; but since pewter is a softer metal than silver, they had to omit some of the more delicate decorations. However, the basic lines remained the same. Black wooden handles and knobs were used with pewter, much as with silver.

I did not begrudge the $30 I paid for the coffeepot made by Gleason, although in the fifties, this seemed quite a bit of money for a coffeepot.

A few years later, I saw a teapot, obviously the mate to my coffeepot, in Bennington Museum in Bennington, Vermont. It was identical in design. I wanted their teapot; they wanted my coffeepot. Stalemate!

There are still many antique shops in Maine, and fine antiques for sale. Perhaps you will find a Gleason teapot; perhaps I will . . .

Two Acres of Antiques

NEW YORK 1948

During the forties, a tremendous sale of antiques took place in New York: several of the William Randolph Hearst collections were offered at Gimbels. A whole floor had been cleared, and where suits or overcoats had been sold, there were now displayed antique bottles, armor complete with halberds, and massive pieces of furniture. There was pewter, brass, and copper; there were old books and paintings. Two acres of antiques; everything neatly tagged; all prices FINAL!

I spent many a lunch hour or late afternoon after working hours examining the enormous accumulation which Hearst had amassed. His agents had roamed all over the world, had bought bottles and jars from old apothecary shops, had purchased carpenters' and cabinetmakers' tools and benches which had not been used in many years. They had acquired wall panellings of old French inns, and even entire English castles.

I examined many fine old books, looked at artisans' tools, and at sets of china, each of which contained hundreds of pieces. I was overcome by the sheer quantity of possessions owned by one man.

There were, of course, many things that I liked, but most things were too large for my use. What could I have done with a set of three hundred pieces of silver? Or with as many glasses for wine, champagne, sherbet, iced tea, etc?

At last, I found something that I had been looking for during the past three years. I had never forgotten how, in the Pennsylvania Dutch country, I had turned down a set of eight goblets of deep aquamarine Baccarat because they were $4 a piece. That was years earlier. Now I saw a much larger set of the same color and quality at half the price. The set contained goblets, dessert dishes, and a large cake stand, all in perfect condition. I also discovered a very fine cut glass decanter which I purchased at once, and which has never since gone dry.

Earlier, during the sale, I had acquired a handsome piece of furniture which I used to house the treasures I bought during those years. It was an old corner cabinet made of pine which I bought from a dealer in a small shop on Third Avenue. That man gave me many interesting pointers on furniture. I began to know what to look for, and not always to expect pure styles, but to be able to compromise and accept furniture which was sound, attractive, and useful for my purposes.

I learned how different woods were used. For instance, the seat of a rocking chair might be made of pine; hickory might be used for the spindles because of the resilience of that wood; and the durability of walnut or oak would be perfect for the rest of the chair.

The corner cabinet I bought formerly had two doors. These had been removed, the hinge marks still showing. Where the doors had been, a scalloped piece of wood had been added on top. The inside of the cabinet was now exposed, and had been painted a grayish blue. Today, one would have to pay over $600 for such a corner cabinet. The price to me then was $90.

This was the first sizeable piece of furniture in our collection. In the years that followed, I found it practical to buy only such furniture for which we had actual use; otherwise, my house would have become a storehouse. In the end, I would have had to become a dealer myself.

That year I bought a Pennsylvania Dutch box which I found at Ginsberg and Levy, a store of great prestige,

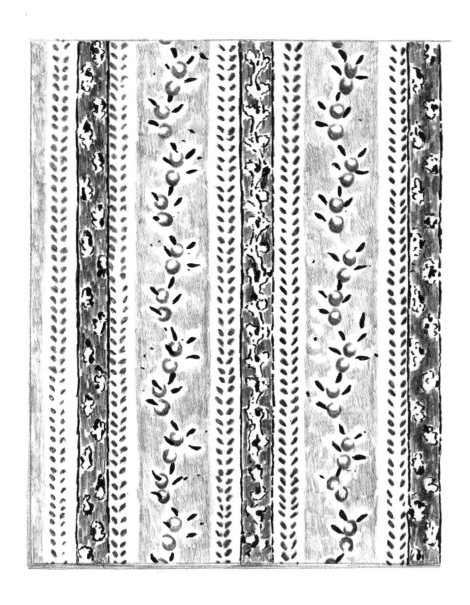

located on 57th Street between Madison and Park Avenue. The box was displayed prominently in the window; it was obvious that it would not be cheap. It was made with the traditional wooden hinges and decorated in the characteristic style of the Pennsylvania Dutch. Years later, I bought another box of this kind, thousands of miles away from New York; and when I came home from Zurich, I found that the Swiss box was identical in its proportions to the Pennsylvania Dutch chest I had.

It was not often that I paid more for antiques than I thought I could afford; but since I had been very careful in my purchases for a long time, I felt that every now and then I could spend a little more than I had planned to. My 57th Street purchase was one of the few times that happened. But I can get five times as much today for that box than the $30 I paid for it.

In those years I was fortunate, for my own work offered constant stimulation. As a book designer, I was forever looking for novel ways of decorating the books I worked on. Though economy was the keynote of book printing, nevertheless, some limited editions were produced which required special efforts in the design of the bindings.

During the 18th and 19th centuries, many books were bound in half leather. This means that the spine, as well as the vulnerable corners of the binding, were covered with leather. The remaining parts of the front and back covers were bound in colorful, handmade papers.

Whenever I could, I searched for remnants of these colorful printed sheets which so often resembled the fine wallpapers of the period. Such papers were also used extensively to bind the many pamphlets of scientific and po-

litical content which were printed during the 18th century in Europe and in America.

One day, while looking at fine books in the shop of Walter Schatzky on Madison Avenue, I discovered a bin which contained many such decorative papers, as well as a quantity of pamphlets. Most of the papers were about two hundred years old. The papers had been decorated in a variety of ways. Some were printed by using diminutive, shaped nails; others, with woodblocks. Some had been embossed with silver or gold leaf, and had been dyed in many colors. More often, these papers had been brushed with paint mixed with paste, a process which made it possible to create original patterns by combing and removing some of the paint.

As it has so often happened in my life when I have been overwhelmed by the beauty of some work of art, I decided then and there to start collecting decorative papers. I made a good start that day, but I have never been able to match the magnificient collection in the Widener Library at Harvard University which contains thousands of the most beautiful hand-decorated papers.

It is hard to beat New York City for the sheer number of its antique shops. Back in the forties, all kinds of antiques were sold in the good shops on Third Avenue, and also in the finest shops on Madison Avenue, and in some galleries on 57th Street and in the 50's in the neighborhood of Park Avenue.

New York City was our headquarters for antiques until we moved to Connecticut. It was naturally easier to explore New England from there, and antique hunting became a happy activity in the years to come.

"An Excellent Restoration Service"

FLORENCE 1950

In some parts of Italy, notably in Tuscany—and especially in Florence, Siena, and Assisi—one is literally surrounded by art treasures. Of course, most of them are in museums or in churches, or they are public monuments. But here and there an antique shop offers a rich choice of furniture and smaller pieces.

In Florence, not far from the Duomo with its famous campanile by Giotto, I found an antique shop which sold beautiful faiences and paintings by unknown masters of the Renaissance. In a small vitrine near the window, a charming little box was displayed. On its cover, there were angels painted in oil. This motif was repeated on only two of the four sides, the painting on the other two having been erased by time or carelessness.

While I thought the box lovely, I was sure that I could find a more perfect example of a *schatolla* elsewhere. Perhaps the imperfection made the box somewhat less appealing. At that time, I was still looking for perfect pieces. Today, I know that the perfect pieces are found, by and large, only in museums, or in great private collections. Perhaps, too, as I have grown older, I find myself more tolerant of the legitimate signs of age.

Still, I picked up the box and asked the price. The suave-looking salesman named a preposterously high figure, par for the course where American tourist meets dealer in Italy.

The young man may have sensed that he was about to lose a sale, and perhaps a customer. Turning to me he said that I must have misunderstood him, and he named a price that was two-thirds of that which he had quoted before. I was still not interested, and I pointed out to him that the design was missing on two sides.

"Oh, that can be remedied," he assured me. "We have an excellent restoration service." I thanked him and edged toward the door, happy to escape.

I believe in restoration per se only where it is absolutely necessary. When such a repair has been made, the dealer should tell you about it and should price the article accordingly.

That afternoon, I returned to the hotel and casually mentioned the matter to my wife. Then I forgot the incident.

A few days later, I was waiting for her to come back from a visit to the dressmaker. At that time, many tourists had dresses made in Florence, shoes in Venice, and handbags in Milan. When my wife entered our room, she had a small package in her hand. She seemed pleased and excited.

"You were so disappointed the other day," she said, "that I hunted for a schatolla in all the antique shops, and I finally found a beautiful one in perfect condition. Here it is!"

I unwrapped the package and there was my little box, angels and all, restored carefully to its original glory. I could not help marvelling at the art of the restorer and the wiliness of the salesman, but I never told my wife.

Florence, with its many art treasures, had indeed in-

69

trigued us. We had visited the Uffizi and the Palazzo Pitti. We had seen Michelangelo's *David*, and the frescoes of Fra Angelico, and much more. Now we journeyed southward across the Arno. We saw Sienna, Assisi, and, finally, the mountain town of San Gimignano.

In this fascinating town, famous for its turret castles and its magnificent view of the Toscana, we discovered a little shop which, surprisingly, specialized in graphic arts. Neatly arranged in deep drawers were many wonderful engravings, some of them by the 18th-century Italian engraver, Giovanni Battista Piranesi. When the owner realized that I was interested in Piranesi, he was pleased. He himself was a collector and completely dedicated to the graphic arts.

The engravings depicted architectural scenes, powerful in line and composition, quite representative of Piranesi's work. The monuments and ruins of ancient Rome and other Italian cities had provided the artist with an unending number of subjects. Three of his engravings, in their black and white austerity, now hang on my walls, providing an interesting contrast to the color of my books and antiques. To think that I bought those engravings for less than $30. All three of them!

EGELLIOLE

Altra Veduta del
tempio della Sibilla
in Tivoli
1 Sustruzioni dell' aja del
tempio dalla parte della
cascata del Teverone.
2 Parte del Tempio sup=
posto d'Albunea.

Piranesi F

All Roads Lead to Innsbruck

INNSBRUCK 1950

All roads lead to Innsbruck. Maybe not all, but quite a few. For centuries, this town, situated in the Austrian Alps, has been a junction of much traffic. When the barbarians invaded Italy, they came from the north, crossed the Alps, and descended upon the fertile flatlands of Italy. On their way to the Holy Land, crusaders from France, England, and Germany traveled through Innsbruck.

Yes, Innsbruck has a rich history. There are castles and there are art treasures; and today, one hears the whistle of the locomotive and the unending trains rolling over the Brenner Pass.

When I was a boy, my family passed through Innsbruck every summer on our way to an Austrian mountain village where we spent our vacations. We would always stop in Innsbruck for a day or two. I was allowed to go sightseeing on my own, during the quiet mid-summer afternoons. I also liked to spend some time in the Café München where I sat at a round marble-topped table, nursing a glass of raspberry soda. For me, the main attraction was a three-man orchestra: a pianist, a violinist, and a cellist. They seemed to know all the music that had ever been written. On every table, there was a little brochure, listing hundreds of pieces of music, each with an identifying number. If the violinist placed the figure 97 facing the patrons, it meant that the orchestra was going to play the *Overture* to *The Barber of Seville*. This, of course, was in the days before radio.

All this came back to me when 33 years later and accompanied by my wife, I found myself back in Innsbruck for the first time since childhood. It was five years after the War, and we had never seen such destruction. Many of the old buildings had been bombed. Where there had once been a wall, we saw a bathtub suspended precariously. There were few automobiles in the streets.

The next day we went for a lengthy walk. We came upon a familiar landmark, a small park which I remembered. The Café München, which had been the scene of so many pleasant concerts in my youth, had been near this park. I tried to find it, but couldn't. When I was about to give up, I noticed a post stuck in the top of a heap of rubble. A number of cards had been nailed onto the post. These cards contained messages and inquiries for missing persons, and also offered information concerning the whereabouts of others. One of the cards said very simply, "Hans Koncert, Antiquitäten." Since street signs were up even where buildings were down, it was not difficult to find the address.

We came upon a small group of houses spared by the bombs, standing lonely amid the rubble. Nailed to the door of one of these houses was a card that read "Hans Koncert, Antiquitäten."

We opened the heavy portal, and found ourselves in a dark courtyard. Walking over the cobblestones, we spotted the card once again which directed us, this time, to walk up to the second floor. The hall and creaky staircase were dark and without a sign of life. We climbed to the second landing where we were barely able to discern the now familiar card on a door. As we pushed the door open, an old-fashioned bell resounded through the unlit rooms. It was eerie. We stood very still, not knowing what to expect next. But in a moment, the lights went on and a pleasant, middle-aged man came forward to greet us.

What we saw in this room took our breath away. Lined against the walls were numerous, beautifully decorated Baroque wardrobes and chests, such as would have been found

in the Austrian villages of the 18th and very early 19th centuries. There were wooden statues and statuettes—angels, saints and madonnas—even entire crèches. There were pewter candlesticks and candle holders, small wooden boxes fashioned like chests which were intended to hold important papers. To find such a treasure of Austrian folk art assembled in a few rooms was a unique experience. It was staggeringly beautiful!

Mr. Koncert explained to us that many of the antiques had belonged to his father, and that other articles, having been "liberated" by soldiers of both the conquering and the conquered armies, had found their way to his shop.

At that moment, I felt I wanted to buy everything in sight, and start an antique shop of my own. Actually, I bought only a few very beautiful pieces, among them a miniature chest with painted decorations.

We also bought a round, painted wooden tub, such as brides in Austrian villages fill with small possessions to be taken along after the wedding. On one of its sides, the tub carried a good-natured admonition to "be happy and industrious." On its other side, the names of the young couple were lettered, as well as the date of the wedding. All of this was shipped home.

After we returned, I regretted not having bought more, and entered into a correspondence with the amiable shop owner. Subsequently, Mr. Koncert sent me photographs and a price list of pewter plates, an octagonal wine carrier used to store wine in taverns, and a magnificent Baroque pewter pitcher of graceful, classic design. I did not hesitate to send for all these articles, for they seemed very beautiful

and very reasonably priced at less than $50. In due time, they arrived in good condition.

Before we left Innsbruck, Mr. Koncert had kindly sent us on to another shop owned by two sisters named Reitmeyer. In contrast to his shop, theirs was, indeed, quite small. We were tired out from working our way through the Koncert shop which had consisted of three or four rooms, and we could see almost immediately that there was not much here to match the larger shop.

Yet we found a prize here—a flying angel with a sweet, childish face. It was beautifully sculptured, and painted in soft flesh tones, with the loincloth and wings richly gilt. The angel had come to grief at one time, and had lost a wing which had been replaced by one of proper size but of a different feather structure. This is a little failing that I overlook, and that has never really bothered me. However, the fault reduced the price to a modest $15.

We packed the angel most carefully in cloth; and we carried it in our arms like a baby throughout the rest of the trip, never even packing it into a suitcase.

The Reitmeyers were dear old ladies who had survived the bombings and were eager to make a living, probably selling their own belongings. When I returned to Innsbruck many years later, I looked for them again but could not find them.

Subsequent visits to the Landeskunst Museum, with all its wonderful treasures, convinced me that mine is worthy of a place among them.

Aldus of Venice

VENICE 1950

When chance took me to Venice for the first time, I was only fifteen years old. On first sight of this fabulous city, I felt that time had stood still. As a boy, I had dreamed of the Middle Ages, of castles and moats, of cathedrals and mosques, of crusaders and galleons, and I had dreamed of Venice.

What I saw made me dizzy! The wondrousness of it all! Here were avenues and streets of water; instead of carriages and automobiles, gondolas glided on canals.

A steady stream of people milled through the squares and narrow lanes and over the many footbridges. No buses, no trolleys, no automobiles. The hotels were converted old Renaissance palazzos, which could be entered from the lanes and also from the canals.

The architecture was magnificent. The houses, having been built at different times over the centuries, were each unlike the other. On the canal side, each house had one or two beautiful striped poles where gondolas could be docked. On the Canale Grande, the entrances from the water side were more elaborate than on the land side. When the sun set, huge and deep red, it was reflected on the Grand Canal and in the windows of the buildings.

As a youngster left to my own devices—for my father had urged me to spend a few days alone in this wondrous city—I walked everywhere, got lost, sat in the outdoor cafés, listened to the music of small, enthusiastic orchestras, and experienced Venice as I have not since.

The beauty of the Piazza San Marco is indescribable. Surrounded by palazzos and by a mosque-like cathedral, it is bordered on the canal side by the Palace of the Doges, a unique edifice, massive with its patterned pink and white marble facade, and elegant white-arched columns. The piazza was at all times crowded with tourists and pigeons. And, of course, it still is.

In later years, I learned to enjoy going to Venice's museums and churches. I also was invited to private homes, and I began to explore the city's fine antique shops and interesting book stores.

I knew that Venice was famous for its glass industry, most of which is housed on the nearby island of Murano. I don't care for those glass pieces which are blown as souvenirs for the tourist trade, although I found a magnificent collection of modern glass at Venini. In Murano, however, which is well worth visiting, I found a unique small museum, housing a glass collection which includes samples of the glass blowers' art dating back over 2,000 years. For anyone who likes glass, this museum is an unforgettable experience.

Near the Rialto in a small square almost hidden by the powerful statue of a man on horseback, the *condottiere Colleoni*, there was an antique shop which attracted my attention. When I opened the door I heard the ringing of several little bells which had been fastened on a leather thong. I looked up with some surprise. The proprietor, leaning against a table, smiled at me. He made me think of Puccini. Perhaps it was the bells; perhaps it was his moustache.

HIERONYMI

RAGAZONII IN

epistolas Ciceronis
familiares

COMMENTARIVS:

IN QVO BREVISSIME, QVO
quæque earum ordine scripta sit, ex ipsa
potissimum historia demonstratur.

AL · DVS.

VENETIIS, M. D. LV
apud Paulum Manutium Aldi F.

83

After browsing around for a while, I found two very small things that hardly seemed to belong in this shop: one, a miniature globe in a tiny paper box; the other, a book bound in paper.

Whenever I have found books in antique shops, they have cost less than in antiquariats. I opened the book to find the familiar dolphin on the title page, the characteristic printers' mark of the early days of printing. The book, almost 500 years old, cost only a few lire. The same was true of the globe, an educational plaything of the early 19th century. The printer of the book, Paolo Manutius, was a nephew of the famous Aldus Manutius, printer and scholar, a name almost as great in the annals of printing as that of Johann Gutenberg.

Old books can be found which are from 400 to 500 years old. The *incunabula* cradle prints of the 15th century are usually well-preserved because they were printed on paper made from rags. Most of these, however, are in libraries and in private collections.

The "black art"—as printing was then called—had quickly spread all over Europe, and eventually to the Americas. In Italy the scholars of the Renaissance were happy to have books other than bibles, missals, and breviaries printed. Johann Gutenberg had made his type resemble the heavy Gothic quill-strokes of the monks and scribes. But soon the Italian printers copied the Roman letter forms they found on the ancient monuments of their country. Still later, "italics" followed, which imitated the free-flowing penmanship of the educated Renaissance man.

As a printer and book designer, well-printed books are of as great interest to me as the antiques with which I have surrounded myself. They stand on the shelves of my library, ever ready to be opened, to be studied, and to be enjoyed.

What did it matter that I slept little that night, kept up till well after midnight by revelling tourists. I had a piece of old Venice for my library. I could look at my globe whenever I wanted to know more about the world.

And I also have a lovely multi-colored glass to remind me that the tradition of art has not died out in Italy. This drinking glass—made by Venini—is one of my prized possessions and would seem to illustrate the old Latin saying, VITE BREVIS / ARS LONGA. Though this glass is not an antique now, I am certain it will be an antique of the future.

The Lake,

and the Bells Ringing in the Sunday

ZURICH 1950

The great mountain and the gorgeous lake, sports events, concerts, art shows, the profusion of flowers, the wonderful shops—all make up the impressive city of Zurich, where in 1950 I spent one glorious summer.

I cannot adequately describe all I saw in the Kunsthalle Museum one Saturday afternoon at the grandiose exhibition "Seven Hundred Years of Iranian Art." There were, among other things, magnificent goblets, pitchers, and other household implements, all made of solid gold, so pure in design they were truly classic. As I ascended the broad steps to the upper hall, Persian temples in life-size photographs rose to the left and right. Never before and never since have I seen rugs as rich in color and as glorious in design as those that were exhibited here.

Sitting on the terrace of my hotel, high above the lake, I heard the church bells of the town ringing in the Sunday. I was still under the spell of what I had seen that day, and the sound of the bells and the setting of the sun filled me with reverence and peace.

The next day, Sunday, I walked through the city without any special purpose. When I left the elegance of the Bahnhofstrasse, past the Seidenhaus Grieder, I found myself in the "Altstadt," the old part of the town which is built solidly around the Limatquai. This is where I found shops with many fine antiques, fairly priced but not bar-

87

gains. There was much to see in the windows, but I had to wait till the next day for the shops to open.

Fortified by a good Swiss breakfast—and where else can one get such rolls as the Swiss *Weggli* served with sweet butter and fresh nutty Emmenthaler cheese and *confiture* —I walked back to explore the shops of the Altstadt.

Good luck was with me. In the first shop I entered, I found so much that I spent the better part of the day there. The owner, an elderly lady with handsome, straightforward features, fascinated me. She had to dispose of two or three customers before she could give me her attention. To the first, she spoke impeccable French; to the second, she addressed herself in the melting tones of Italian; and with the third, without the least effort, she spoke Swiss-German, a dialect I can understand if spoken slowly. She switched from one tongue to the other without a moment's hesitation. I was wondering in what language she would speak to me; but it turned out I was to address her first, so I decided to speak English to her. She answered in the clear British of continental Europeans who have studied in England. Finally, she and I were speaking High German, in which we both were completely at ease. All this was fun, and it was clear that she was a truly accomplished linguist.

I bought a lovely assortment of antiques, the best was a box with a wooden hinge such as I had seen on many painted Pennsylvania Dutch boxes, one of which I had the good fortune to acquire in New York.

The Swiss box was painted in gay colors: blue, red, green, and yellow in the manner characteristic of Alpine primitive artists. The back, however, had been finished in a perfunctory manner with but a few lines and dots. I am

89

convinced that the artist felt that boxes would be placed against a wall, probably on a chest of drawers, and that he might as well save himself the effort of decorating all four sides.

These boxes, made of a whitewood such as birch or ash, are neatly nailed together, not dove-tailed as would have been done by a cabinetmaker, are obviously the products of simple country folk. Such an artist could always be found in most villages, because much decorative work needed to be done. Furniture, such as a *Bauernschrank*, and chests were decorated, as were farm implements. Walls were painted and decorated, and so too were the outsides of many houses and barns. Tools carried decorative carving, and all metals were forged and cast with an eye for beauty. The homes of prosperous peasants or shopkeepers might contain enough furniture and smaller pieces to fill a small museum of folk art.

It was my day for buying wooden articles. When I left the store, the box for which I gladly paid 50 Swiss francs (about $12) was filled with two square wooden molds, customarily used for Christmas cakes or marzipan. One of the molds was carved with a trumpeter on horseback; the other, with an ensign on horseback. The soldiers were done in the realistic manner of the 19th century. Today, they rank among my favorite pieces. I was almost embarrassed to buy them for $4 apiece.

Whether intentionally or not, I have always bought antiques that I could use. The Swiss box would house important papers; the molds would come in handy around the holidays. Molding marzipan is not difficult; but since marzipan is very oily when the ground almonds are still

fresh, the mold must be powdered with confectioner's sugar. If such a mold is used with shortbread, the wood should be powdered with flour.

My talented shopkeeper had to make a separate package of three Christmas balls which I purchased but which had been overlooked. Their combined colors—deep blue, blood red, and silver—were absolutely gorgeous. They were quite expensive but I did not bargain; it was love at first sight.

The shop owner promised to wrap the painted box carefully and ship it to America. Shipping antiques by boat takes a long time—never less than six weeks, usually more.

Waiting for your antiques is an emotional trial, but there's a reward too, for what can be nicer than to open

the door when the postman rings bearing a large package from abroad. After you have unwrapped your treasure and found a worthy place for it, you sit back and make plans for still another treasure quest.

"Sold to the Gentleman

from the Big City"

NEW HAMPSHIRE 1952

The farm auction was in full swing. Apparently the contents of the farmhouse had been auctioned off the day before, and now followed the contents of the barn and the big farm implements.

It was fascinating to hear the rural auctioneer who was witty and as fast as lightning. It seemed to us that he could sell anything to anyone; we hoped we would not be tempted to bid on a hay wagon or a pitchfork.

The auctioneer then picked up an article or two from the table, but he didn't get any bids. He turned to the crowd and grinned, yelling, "Who will give me ten cents for the lot?"

Some jokester yelled back, "More goods!"

The auctioneer picked up what was left—an old-fashioned coffee mill fell back on the table—his arms were full, and he disposed of the entire lot for twenty cents. He then picked up the old coffee mill by its handle, and holding it aloft cried, "What am I bid for a beautiful antique coffee mill?"

The crowd laughed good-naturedly. I stood up, raised my arm, and shouted over the din, "Five cents!"

The auctioneer smiled at me and said, "Sold to the gentleman from the big city for five cents!" Then he pulled out a big red handkerchief from his pocket, and wiping his

96

tired, sweaty face, walked away leaving the settling to his assistants.

That was almost thirty years ago. The coffee mill is still with me, and sometimes we use it to grind coffee. When we do, I again see the crowd at the auction, drinking coffee and at long tables eating the apple pie sold by the neighbors' wives.

That same summer, we went to another auction. This one took place in a small warehouse in Laconia. Most of the articles were furniture; some of them were little used but not very attractive. The furniture not in perfect condition was auctioned off *as is*, and had to be paid for and taken away immediately. This, of course, presented problems. We had no car, yet we were determined to find another bargain, even if we had to spend more than a nickel.

As usual, the auction began in the morning. Around lunchtime, sandwiches and coffee, as well as blueberry pie, were available. To keep the spirits of the children up and their voices down, parents bought them Eskimo pies.

An attendant walked up and down the middle aisle, showing articles which were about to be auctioned off. By the time an article was placed on the auctioneer's table, another item had made its way back and forth along the aisle. It was like parading slave girls in ancient Rome to entice the customers at a slave auction.

Number "77" was a black rocker with a faint trace of the old, gold stencil. The thin gold stripes painted on the delicate armrests were virtually extinct. All the same, it looked like a nice chair, even though one of the spindles was missing and another was broken.

The rocker was offered for $10. The auctioneer coun-

98

tered the silence that answered his proposal with a plea to the customers to realize how hard it was to find Windsor rockers "these days." He offered the chair again, this time for $5. Someone offered $2. The bidding became lively. Two women bid each other up to $4, 25¢ at a time. The auctioneer looked disgusted. He half turned to call his assistant to bring something else. After a one-second consultation with my wife, I boldly offered $5. The ladies withdrew. I had won. Some people snickered.

Had I known then how much it would cost me to get the rocker crated, shipped, refinished, and the spindles replaced; had I known that there would be still more to repair, I might have remained silent. But the rocker is still one of the finest pieces of furniture in my home.

The auction was over; people began to drift away; furniture was loaded onto station wagons. While we waited around, I noticed a pile of furniture which had been consigned to a junk pile. I browsed idly, turning a piece here and there.

When I opened the door of an old-fashioned medicine cabinet whose gingerbread decorations had been broken off and one side of which had been caved in; I noticed something colorful. It turned out to be a part of an old broadside. The captions were quite legible and amusing. The piece heralded the concert tour of Jenny Lind arranged by P. T. Barnum. I tried to remove the broadside, but it was pasted tightly to the inside of the door.

Just then the auctioneer happened to be passing by. I asked him about the chest. He told me to help myself. One hinge of the door was already missing, and it did not require much of an effort to twist the other hinge off the cabinet.

When we returned to the tourist home where we were staying, I submerged the little door in a few inches of warm water in the bathtub. A few hours later, the door and the colorful broadside parted company. I dried the print between blotting paper which I borrowed from the writing desk in the parlor. Our landlady had watched the proceedings with some suspicion; but when she saw the illustrations, still damp but in good condition, she exclaimed, "My, it's pretty! Why do you suppose they pasted it inside a medicine chest?" I told her we would probably never find out.

The next day we drove to a small town near Wolfeboro at Lake Winnipesaukee. A store in the main square carried the sign "Antiques." What was surprising was that the window was filled with canned groceries and fresh vegetables and that there was a sign over the entrance door which read "U. S. Post Office." Next to it hung an American flag.

Inside the store were more groceries and a butcher's counter. Customers were being helped, but no antiques were to be seen. Opposite the counter, there was a door and a little closed window above which hung another small sign identifying it as a U. S. Post Office. The whitewashed walls were covered with postal announcements and small WANTED signs. I knocked at the window. It was opened for me. Behind the window, an elderly man was comparing an old-fashioned bottle to an illustration in an open book. The bottle was shaped like a violin. I felt that I was getting closer to the antiques.

The postmaster explained that when he was taking care of postal business, the antique shop upstairs—he pointed

Die Amerikaner sitzen nicht, sie stehen nicht
während der Vorstellung der Jenny Lind son,
dern sie knien vor ihr und bethen sie an.

Herr Barnunn der Theaterdirector geleitet die Nachtigal
des Nordens, Abends in ihre Behausung. Er schliesst
sie in einen goldenen Käfig ein.

to the ceiling with his forefinger—was closed; and if he were busy with a customer upstairs, people would have to wait for their stamps. The grocery shop was taken care of

102

by his wife. He closed the window, and then he took me up a dark staircase to his antique shop.

He had many old bottles, but I particularly liked a square pint bottle which had been used for gin. It was rarer than the quart-size bottle, and of course, it was empty. There was also a small whiskey bottle in the same condition, decorated on one side with the traditional cornucopia and on the other, a vase with flowers. Both bottles were olive green and cost $2.50 each.

When I inquired about the violin bottle which he had

been examining in the post office, he hesitated. He was reluctant to sell that, mumbled something about, "Thought I would give it to Mabel." In the end, he took the $4 I offered. I was glad to have that violin-shaped bottle, for such bottles are not easy to find.

A transom permitted the postmaster to look downstairs and see that a number of people were patiently standing in line before the post office window. He became nervous, and tried to bring our business to an end. Just before we went down the stairs, I noticed a little white plaque with relief portraits of three young girls. The plaque was made of plaster-of-Paris. The style of the girls' hairdos indicated that the plaque was a half-century old. I inquired of him whether he knew who the girls were. He said, "The one in the middle was Aunt Mabel. It's yours for a dollar." He wrapped it quickly and added, "The old lady didn't want to admit that it was her with her sisters. She said it dated her too much."

Strange, how one acquires lovely things, and how it sometimes takes time to examine them and to appreciate them fully. But isn't that the way with so many possessions we have? It was years later when someone pointed out to me that two of the girls on the plaque had tiny wings growing out of their shoulders. We wondered if that indicated that they were dead when the portrait was made (perhaps from a photograph). Or could it be that the girls had seemed like angels to their parents? I am afraid we'll never know.

A Small Box in Storage House "B"

BERLIN 1955

As the plane broke through the low lying clouds, I saw my home town in ruins. The roofs were burnt out, and what had been the avenues and squares of Berlin were now fields of rubble.

I took a room in a small hotel in the suburb of Charlottenburg where I grew up. Charlottenburg is in the residential section of the Kurfürstendamm. The first thing I did was to walk through the streets. Many blocks had disappeared entirely, but street signs were there. Here and there a house stood, undistinguished architecturally but just as familiar to me as it had been 25 years earlier. In some cases, the bricks of a destroyed house were piled up neatly; other residences were now just mounds of rubble.

The next morning I took a taxi directly to the office of a warehouse. I had come to inquire about what had been stored there by my parents many years ago.

An old man helped me go through records, lists, bills and receipts, opening files in one room or another until he could tell me, with the characteristic German love for detail, where our goods could be found. "Most of them," he said, "had unfortunately been in *Storage House E*, the one that had been entirely destroyed. The gentleman, your father," he said, glancing at the papers, "did not carry any special insurance that would cover the loss."

I angrily replied that my father could not have foreseen

that his furniture might be consumed by the flames of a war which had its very origin in this city. Fortunately, my parents had moved to Hungary years before the advent of the Third Reich.

The old man looked out of the window, saying nothing. He probably had heard such talk before. After a while he looked at the papers again and said, "I notice that there is a small box belonging to your father in *Storage House B*. Since that building was relatively unharmed, we may be able to find the box." He offered to take me there, and we found the box undamaged.

A worker carried it to the office. The old man looked at the clock and said, "Lunch time! Come back at two o'clock if you like." Lunch time is a holy institution the world over, and I knew that this man had worked for the same company for over fifty years and had lived under the Monarchy, the Republic, and the Dictatorship, surviving them all. He would take his lunch time, no matter what.

At two o'clock sharp, I reported back. I felt like a schoolboy standing at attention before a strict teacher. He showed me a list of items contained in the box. A number of them did not interest me particularly. There were some individual plates—not entire sets. There were small, framed photo-

Der Böhmische Borsdorfer.

Die Holländische Rietbirn.

graphs, presumably family portraits, also some napkins and tablecloths. But there were two things that *did* attract my attention.

The list read, "Collection of 14 colored prints." Also miscellaneous *nippes*, a word as horrible as its translation *knick-knacks*. Yet every family had nippes.

I asked him to open the box, but the old man wanted to know first if I had a Power of Attorney from "the gentleman, your father." I told him, curtly, that my father had died twenty years before, and that I was his sole heir. He seemed to understand.

Now he insisted that I would have to pay accumulated charges before I took possession. I replied that I would certainly not pay for anything they had carelessly allowed to be destroyed, but if he wished, he could charge me for this particular box. Whether he thought that this was just, or whether he didn't care what happened to the tiny remnants of a family's possessions, or whether he just wanted to get rid of me, I don't know. The storage charges on one small box were very low; but multiplied by the number of years during which no payments had been made, it added up.

Finally, the box was opened. After I paid my father's bill, we took out everything. The linens did not look usable, and some of the plates were cracked. The photographs were probably of relatives and friends of my parents; I could not identify any of them.

The prints—they depicted fruit such as apples, pears, grapes, figs and even walnuts—were beautiful. Hand-colored realistically but with sophistication, they had been produced by using a delicate, dotted outline of the fruit with stems and leaves. Each print had been colored by several artists who followed the original painting with great accuracy. For instance, in doing an apple, the first artist might fill in the guidelines with yellow; the second artist would add a blush of red; the third would paint the stems and leaves green; the fourth would add delicate shading; and the fifth, perhaps the highlights. This method preceded color separation by camera by almost a century. One print was made at a time. Working in this manner, perhaps not more than a thousand prints of any painting were produced. Prints of these old paintings are often reproduced by printing methods, and are passed off as originals to fool the unschooled eye.

At the end of my visit to the warehouse, I was exhausted. Somehow I felt the misery of recent history in all its turmoil. I left the box—wrapping paper and all—taking only the fruit prints and a little porcelain figurine of a small boy sitting on a bench and drinking his milk from a little white mug. When I was a child I had innocently assumed that I was that little boy, or rather that the little porcelain figure was a portrait of me.

In later years, when I visited a ceramics factory in Copenhagen, I discovered that that particular figurine of the little boy was still being manufactured. That very day I saw a batch of 300 newly-produced milk-drinking boys on a large table waiting to be packaged and shipped.

Casa Serodine

ASCONA 1955

In the Canton Ticino, at the foothills of the Swiss Alps to the north, and connected with Italy by the Lago Maggiore, lies Ascona. In former years little more than a fishing village, it has become a favorite tourist spot in our time. Homes and hotels border the lake and climb the hills. The locale is southern, more Italian than Swiss. Small *vaporetti* steam up and down the lake, and far beyond the border which cuts the blue waters in two.

In the center of Ascona lies an old walled monastery. The Casa Serodine, a Baroque palazzo, stands not far from the lake terrace with its rows of chestnut trees—so characteristic of European lake fronts.

No sign will tell you that this well preserved building is crammed full of antiques. Yet, the heavy oaken portals are wide open during the day, and people walk in and out of the building. So there should be no question in anybody's mind about the nature of this grand edifice, especially since one can see stone statuary through the wide entrance.

We did not hesitate to enter, and were soon busy examining and admiring the contents of the three floors built around a courtyard. There was so much to see: furniture, glass, metalcraft, books, and graphic arts were mixed in colorful profusion.

We admired the primitive furniture, beautiful and

readily available in Europe, but so expensive to crate and ship, to say nothing of the problem of finding enough space in your home to house some of these massive things.

There were, of course, many angels and *putti* (cherub heads with wings), as well as wooden sculptures of saints. Much of the material that one can buy in Switzerland was saved from the hand of irate iconoclasts during the Reformation, and has wound up in antique shops, usually in a state of good preservation. Naturally, much of it has found its way to museums and private collections, and has often been used to decorate fine hotels. The contents of the Casa

Serodine had originally been housed in an antique shop in Vienna. The Austrian owner had moved all his possessions to Zurich, and eventually to the serenity of Ascona.

We found wooden sculptures of two of the apostles, barely five inches high, with their original paint, depicting in great detail St. Peter with his key and St. Paul with his sword. Such sculptures were part of groups of the twelve apostles. The two statuettes we bought in the Casa Serodine were too small to have come from a church, so I presume that they had once graced the home of a peasant family. We were happy to get them at around $15 for the pair.

It should be said that an inexperienced buyer of antiques is best off going to a good shop where prices may not be bargain prices but where the owner is knowledgeable and honest. This was true at the Casa Serodine whose owner, an art expert, knew a great deal more than many shop owners whom I have met. It is never easy to find "sleepers," articles of a higher value than that set by a not-too-knowledgeable owner.

In another room, we browsed through the contents of several portfolios and found, to our great pleasure, pages from a Book of Hours of the 15th century with charming illustrations from the Bible. There was also an etching of some Dutch ships of war of the 17th century, and a master

WHollar fecit.

Anthoni pastor incli
te qui cruciatosreficis
morbos sanas & de
struis ignis calore ex
tinguis pr̄ q es supis
ora p nobis dn̄m: vt
celū nobis miseris do
net post vite terminū. ℣. Ora p no
bis btē pr̄ anthoni ℟. Vt digni. oℜ,
Eus q nos cōcedis obtētu bea
ti āthonii cōfessoris tui morbī
du igne extigui:& mēbris egris re
frigeria p̄stari:fac nos ip̄ius meritis
& p̄cibus a gehēne icēdiis liberatos
itegros mēte & corpe tibi feliciter i
glia p̄sētari.p. De sc̄tō rocho. ān.
Aue roche sc̄tissie nobili nat⁹ lan
guine crucissignarisscemate sinistro
tuo latere. Roche pegre p̄fectuspe
stis fere curastactatus egros sanans
mirifice tāgēdo salutifere. Vale ro
che angelice vocis citat⁹ famie/q po
tēs es deifice a cūctis peste pellere
℣. O ra p nobis btē rocheℜ. Vt me
reamur preseruari a peste. ℗ Oℝō

Eus q btō rocho p āgelū tuū
tabulā e. dē afferētē p̄misisti vt
q ipsū pie iuocauerit a nullo pestis
cruciatu lederet:p̄sta q̄svt q e⁹ mēo
riā agimus:ip̄ius meritis a mortife
ra peste corpis et aīe leberemur. p,
De sancto fiacro, aña, Beate xp̄i
cōfessor fiacri:ecce nomē tuū fulget
per secula:petimus ergo tuis sacris
precibus iuuari mereamur ℟, Ora p
nobis btē pr̄ fiacri, ℟. Vt digni, Oℜ.
Iser icordiā tuā nobis dn̄e iter
ueniēte beato fiacro cōfessore
tuo clemēter ipēde:& nobis pctōri
bus ip̄ius p̄piciare suffragiis, Per,
De sc̄tā anna. Aña.,
Aue mater mr̄is dei
per quā salui fiūt rei:
aue p̄le fecū data āna
deo dedicata:pro fide
li plebe tota apd chri
stū sis deuota,℣ Ora
p nobis btā āna, ℟. Vt digni, Oℝō.
Eus q btē āne tātā grā̄ dona
re dignatus es:vt b̄tissimā vn

certificate for a German draper, dated 1789. All of these ephemera now hang on our walls.

Printed Books of Hours are rare, although now and then, one runs across individual pages. I recognized that the ships were Dutch by the pennants they were flying, and the peculiarly Dutch manner of depicting ships in meticulous detail.

The master certificate, quaintly worded and printed with flourish, was at one time—perhaps two hundred years

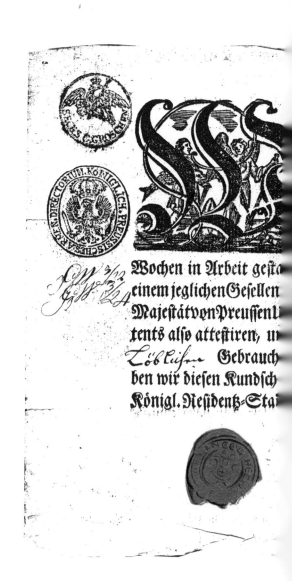

ago—as common as the diplomas you see in doctors' offices today. To save further expense, we framed all of these ourselves.

For the last twenty years, ever since I first found the Casa Serodine, I have received invitations to concerts, art shows, and cocktail parties taking place in this unusual house. The owner, who faithfully sends these notices to me, expects me to hop the next plane and attend. I wish I could.

A Town of Music,

Art, and Pastry Shops

VIENNA 1955

I don't know why it is, but whenever I visit a foreign city I lose myself and my available time just walking through the streets and parks and museums.

A few days before my departure from Vienna, I found that I had neglected a good deal. I had not yet attended the opera or even a concert, nor had I found a single antique which I could cherish.

Late one afternoon, I left the Albertina Museum where I had examined, for one glorious day, compositions by Mozart and Haydn written in their own hands. At the entrance door there was a poster announcing a concert to be given the next afternoon. The program included flute concerti by Haydn, Mozart, as well as by Pleyel, a little-known Austrian composer of the same period. I went down to the small box office and asked for a ticket, only to be told that the concert was sold out. I felt crushed.

As I was about to descend the staircase, an attendant in uniform addressed me, asking if there was something he could do for me. I replied that I had hoped to go to the concert and found it had been sold out.

"Oh, the gentleman could come to the next concert," he offered. "We have one every Saturday afternoon." To which I replied that I had to leave for Switzerland the next day. He suggested coming back early on Saturday morning because someone might return a ticket.

On my way back to the hotel, I stopped at a small

antique shop in the Kärntnerstrasse. It was nearing closing time, and for a while I studied a framed music manuscript page. It was signed by Joseph Haydn, and was charmingly written. One could actually *see* the gaiety of the music.

But alas! it was extravagantly priced. I glanced briefly around. There were nice things in the shop, but the owner seemed impatient to close. I probably didn't impress him as a serious customer.

The next morning—it was a lovely, sunny day—I was up early, had breakfast, and went to the Albertina. Scarcely had I walked into the entrance hall when the old attendant rushed over to me, and pulling a ticket out of his pocket, handed it to me, saying, "My dear sir, I am so happy you can go to the concert now. I didn't want you to go back to

your beautiful homeland without hearing a concert in our wonderful museum."

I found this experience so heart-warming, for it was a service rendered without any thought of return. He just wouldn't accept a tip. I thanked him and left the building in great spirits and decided to pay the little antique shop another visit. This time I was not in a hurry, and neither was the owner of the shop. When he realized that I was serious, he showed me some things I had not seen the day before. There were candle holders made of brass and candle holders made of glass. There were samplers, tiles, little wooden sculptures, and much more.

Almost immediately I noted two small angels, each holding a tiny candlestick. They were as charming a pair

as ever graced the side of a small crèche, and were about six inches high. Carved out of pear wood, each standing on a little wooden base, their garments were painted red; their cloaks, green. The wings and the candlesticks they held were gilded, although the wing tips matched the green of the cloak. The whole little sculpture, though carved roughly, had been done with the great skill characteristic of the Austrian woodcarvers of the 18th and 19th centuries. Every village had a wood carver, a truly dedicated, primitive artist who provided churches, monasteries, and homes with wooden figurines. These sculptures were used for crèches and stood at the sides of crucifixes and holy pictures.

Such a picture hung, indeed, between the angels! How could I have overlooked this touching painting depicting a madonna, holding on each arm replicas of herself, complete with halos. The owner of the shop explained to me that this was a *Maria Selbstdritt*—Mary, herself, three times over. I had first thought of it as Trinity, but could not understand why the three figures were identical. I was told that the figures represented Mary, Anna (the mother of Mary), and Elizabeth (the mother of Anna). I examined the picture with great interest, finding it to be painted under glass, and the product of this primitive impractical method is charming for that reason.

The technique is both simple and complicated. Whatever an artist normally paints last, must be painted first; and whatever he usually paints first, must be painted last. This means that eyes, mouths and noses must be indicated on the back of the glass; and even a slight flush on the cheeks must be painted before the flesh color of the face is applied. Not many of these under-glass paintings have survived, undamaged.

Considering all that, I felt the price of $25 was justified. The gracious events of the morning had made me quite happy and entirely willing to buy the sweet little angels. I did then what I think is important in the unending quest for treasures. I stopped looking. I was satisfied.

What a wonderful concert it was! Afterward, I dined as one can only dine in Vienna—on *Tafelspitz*, *Gewürztraminer* and *Sachertorte*. I took a long walk on the Opernring and the Graben. Later, in the Hotel Sacher, I had my small cup of black coffee, and I wished I could stay in Vienna forever.

Vienna! This is where my father grew up and became a musician. Vienna, still the glorious town of great music, fine art, and pastry shops.

It's an Old Flemish Custom

BRUGES 1967

The Flemish are a brave people. Under the Spanish yoke in the Middle Ages, never happy with the French or with the Walloons, and not very close to the Dutch whose language they speak, the Flemish have had need for both courage and ingenuity to survive. It was here that the famous prankster Tyl Ulenspiegel, immortalized in Richard Strauss' tone poem, lived and died.

The Flamands were shrewd traders, fine artisans, and magnificent artists. The Northern Renaissance which produced painters such as Memling, Rogier van der Weyden, van Dyck, Bosch, and Gerard David was centered here. Both Breughels, father and son, recorded faithfully for all time, life in Flanders.

The *tinterrien*, a pewter tureen, that was offered to me in an antique shop on the cobble-stoned square of Brugge not far from the picturesque canals of the town might have come straight out of Pieter Breughel's painting of a village feast. Perhaps the tinterrien was as old as the painting. It probably was used at wedding feasts. With its purchase, I received a description of a Flemish wedding feast which was no less colorful than Breughel's paintings.

"When there was a wedding in the village," said the dealer while he showed me the hallmarks at the bottom of the large pewter serving dish, "everybody in the village was invited. Everybody brought roasted geese and chickens, boiled and roasted meats, fish and smoked eels, vegetables and gravies, cakes and cheeses. They brought wine and beer, cider and milk; and finally, they brought themselves and their families. Everybody ate all there was, down to the last sausage.

"But," said the dealer, lifting his index finger and holding it close to my face for greater emphasis as he paused for effect.

"What happened then?" I filled in, as I knew I was expected to. "Such a feast must have taken a long time!"

"A whole day!" confirmed the dealer. "And when they could eat or drink no more—even though they had gone into the bushes all day long—a big tureen full of gruel served with *sirop* was set before them on the table, and everybody was obliged to eat from it. When any guest could not lift his spoon any longer, he was made to get on the table and sit in the gruel!

"You may be sure the other guests had their fun with him," he went on with the air of a father telling his son the facts of life, "but by that time, the gruel had cooled and didn't raise blisters on his skin."

He winked at me, and I bought the dish with great enthusiasm, and for not too much money—only about $25 in Belgian money. A big pewter ladle, probably used every day for soup and dumplings, came with my tinterrien as an unlooked-for bonus!

This happened four years ago. Today, the two pieces couldn't be bought for five times as much.

Haymarket and Fleamarket

LONDON 1955

"You will find me readily enough," said Peter Parlay, representative of a large printing plant in London. "We are near Covent Garden." As a book designer for an American publishing house, I wanted to use the opportunity of a visit to England to see how books were printed there.

However, I did not find him readily. The neighborhood around Covent Garden, London's opera house, is picturesque and worth exploring. Known as Haymarket, the little section near the Strand in London used to be the marketplace for Londoners of a bygone day; and Covent Garden is now a wholesale-produce district.

The streets in this section are narrow; and the little houses pasted closely together have steep staircases, one of which took me up to Peter's office.

When I entered, I found Parlay seated comfortably at his desk, his long legs propped up on a stack of manuscripts which were placed on the only chair I could see. He was telephoning someone, and motioned me to sit down. I looked around and found a pile of dusty books which served me as a seat. His secretary inquired, sweetly, how we wanted our tea.

"Perhaps you'd care for a crumpet or a scone, sir," she suggested. I felt very much at home, although it seemed the strangest office I had been in, in a long time.

Eventually, Peter Parlay finished his call and rose to

greet me most cordially. He was six foot three, a handsome man with dark hair and a military moustache. He was dressed in grey flannels, a dark jacket, a light blue shirt with a stiff collar, and he wore the traditional tie of the R.A.F. He made me as comfortable as possible, transferring the manuscripts to the floor. After we had had our tea and crumpets, we discussed our business and decided that the next day we would visit the Company's "works."

"We'll motor," he said, cheerily. "Pick you up at your hotel at eight in the morning." We rose. He brushed off the dust that had settled on my suit, and I descended the creaky old staircase into the sunny street. I looked around briefly for antique shops but saw none in this antique neighborhood.

The next morning it was raining hard. Peter was waiting for me in the lobby. He explained we would have to hurry to catch the 8:32 train, as he didn't think I would be comfortable in his open two-seater. We took a taxi to the station and settled ourselves in a train compartment. We were alone and, thus, very comfortable, since these compartments hold six. All had happened so quickly that I had not had time for breakfast. At that moment, the door was opened, and a waiter appeared, offering a breakfast tray complete with eggs, bacon, tea, toast and marmalade. The meal was like a dream. It could not have tasted better!

The trip through the English countryside was uneventful, for the rain prevented me from enjoying the scenery. We had a good time discussing books and printing. From the description that Peter gave me, I realized that the printing plant would be considerably more grand than his office.

I was not disappointed. The plant proved to be very

well-equipped, indeed. It was run in an orderly fashion which was very impressive. I soon lost myself in the many interesting details such a plant has to offer. Peter had delegated a young man to show me the machinery and the library where finished books were on view. He told me he would be busy until lunch time. I had seen a great deal, and I thought I'd like to take a walk through the town. Though the rain had stopped, the clouds still hung very low. I left the plant without informing Peter, whom I hesitated to interrupt.

Bath is a typical English provincial town. It is sufficiently far enough from London to be leisurely in pace. It is neither an industrial nor a college town. The first thing I saw was one of the old crescents, a double row of connected houses built on the north and south sides of an oval park. Such crescents are very common in England, dating back to the time of George III. The houses were built one by one, the builder taking orders after displaying the first sample building, which was well-furnished to please the prospective buyer—a model home of the 18th century.

Continuing my walk through various neighborhoods, I arrived at a marketplace. Outdoor European markets are always fascinating to me, whether what is sold is food or flowers or a variety of merchandise. This particular market sold everything. I went from stand to stand, looking at many things which I did not need, until I came to one which had old brass and copper for sale. It looked like a tinker's stall with its kettles and frying pans, bellows and bed warmers, but all were either too large for me to take along or were in poor condition.

At last, I found a small brass plaque with a raised

alphabet on it, very much of the period of the houses I had admired before. I turned it over and read on the other side, "Bath Orphanage, 1805." "A foine piece, Guvnor," said the old woman who sold it to me, but she could not shed any light on the use of the alphabet. However, before I got back to the plant, I had it figured out. The plaque, presumably one of many cast in brass, had served as a primer for children learning to read. It could be hung conveniently on a nail in a schoolroom; unlike a schoolbook, it could not be easily damaged. There was even a loop by which it could be hung on a nail.

While I had walked up and down the Market Square, I noticed a second-hand bookstore. Out of sheer habit I went in. I discovered a *Euclid, Principles of Geometry*, which made my book designer's heart beat faster. It was printed in four colors, and I could see at a glance what had escaped me in eighth grade, namely, why some angles or distances were identical and how to prove a theorem. The printer of this Euclid—it was published in 1847 in London—had used black ink for all of the text and for some parts of the diagrams; other parts of the diagrams were printed in deep yellow, red, and blue. This was a book that might cause a pupil to love geometry! Q.E.D. Together, the alphabet and the book had cost $11.

I set out next morning to explore Mayfair. A few streets between Hyde Park and Green Park provide antique shops during the day, restaurants in the evening, and night life at night. In Mayfair, I came upon a shop belonging to a very elegant young man, not at all a typical dealer but more likely a participant in the local night life. It turned out, however, that he was very well-informed; and I am

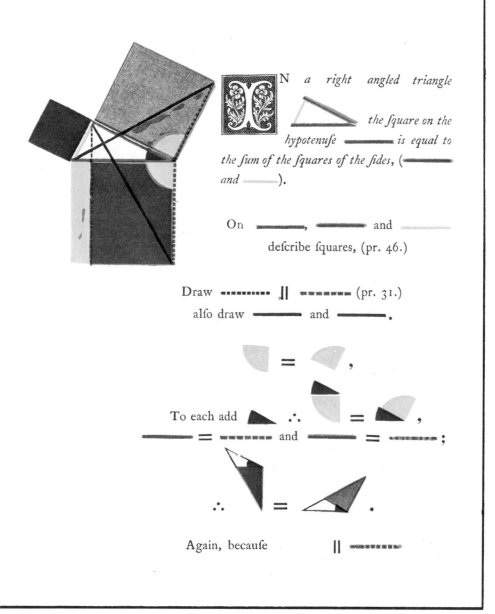

IN *a right angled triangle the square on the hypotenuse* ———— *is equal to the sum of the squares of the sides,* (———— *and* ————).

On ————, ———— and ———— describe squares, (pr. 46.)

Draw •••••••• ‖ ———— (pr. 31.)
alfo draw ———— and ————.

= ,

To each add ∴ = ,
———— = •••••••• and ———— = •••••••• ;

∴ = .

Again, becaufe ‖ ••••••••

indebted to him for much information regarding English, Irish, and French pewter. I was able to buy from him the very thing I had wanted so badly: a well-matched set of six English measures from a quart down to a quarter of a gill. Some hallmarks differ, but the design for tavern measures is pretty uniform. These pieces all bore the royal assayer's mark to prove that none had a false bottom and that each measure was true and honest. Today, the pint measure alone would cost as much as what I paid for the entire set: $40.

To assemble a complete set, dealers patiently wait until they can find individual measures as needed. This is because the measures were made in almost identical patterns

and sold individually to tavern keepers. Similar measures made in France are of a plain cylindrical design and marked in *litres* or *decilitres*. The purpose and the method are much the same. In Ireland, measuring cups were made in the

shape of haystacks, by which name they are commonly called.

In the same shop, I also bought a pair of matched square-bottomed brass candle holders, each of which has an ingenious hidden device to push out the candle stubs.

From Mayfair, it was only a short ride on a double-decker to the much heralded Brompton Road. I will resist a temptation to talk about Harrod's, as fine a department store as any I have seen in Europe, for I must tell you about Casimir's Pewter Shop. The shelves were filled with polished pewter. There were measures, tankards, wine containers, chargers, deep dishes, flat dishes, coffee and teapots, candle holders, candlesticks, inkwells, spoons, cups, and what-have-you.

While English pewter is usually polished, such parts as cannot be seen are left untouched. American pewter, on the other hand, is left entirely unpolished, thus acquiring a lovely, soft gray patina. In England, pewter looks almost like silver, which was, of course, what the pewterers of the 18th and early 19th centuries wanted to accomplish. People who wanted silver but couldn't afford to buy it had to be satisfied with pewter.

In colonial America, English aristocrats and traders could afford silver; colonists, trappers and farmers could not.

Casimir's prices were high, but his pewter was of museum caliber. It was a privilege to see so many things under one roof. In the end, I made an exception and I paid more for a piece than I ordinarily would have. I put my theory of patient waiting aside for as long as it took me to write a check for a lovely covered tureen which I did not buy as an investment, but simply because I did not want to go home without it.

Linares In the Snow

and Linares In the Sun

MADRID AND SEVILLE 1958

A hasty look at the old-fashioned clock in the lobby of the Palace Hotel in Madrid made me realize that I had slept well into the morning. If I wanted to explore the Prado, I had better do without breakfast. So, from the lobby I rushed out into the snowy street, without going back to my room to put on an overcoat. After all, it was only two blocks to the Museum.

The cold air invigorated me. I walked fast; and I told myself I was enjoying a new experience starting the day in this spartan manner. I realized I only had two days left in which to explore both the Museum and the city of Madrid.

The Prado was everything I had expected it to be. There were enormous, colorful Velazquez', the fantastic art of Hieronymous Bosch, some of the hauntingly beautiful elongated figures of El Greco, and oh! so many wonderful Goyas.

Some of the earlier, gayer paintings of Goya which I saw in the Prado were new to me, except, of course, the two *Majas*. When I walked up to the second floor to see his sketches—the work of a man whose mind was already in its twilight—I was spellbound and could hardly move on to the next rooms.

I felt the need for food, but by the time I found the refreshment stand, it was closed. I comforted myself with the thought of a good dinner at the Hotel. Actually, I was a little apprehensive, knowing that dinner is rarely served before ten o'clock in Spain; but the afternoon wore on, and it was four o'clock—closing time—before I knew it. In those years, there were no lights in this Museum, so it had to be closed at sundown.

When I got out into the street, it was much colder than in the morning. The snow had virtually stopped. I rushed towards the lighted Palace Hotel when I realized I was passing an antique shop. And I just never pass an antique shop. Besides, I was so cold that I was glad to walk into the attractive three-story building.

At once I was aware that it was one of the finest shops I had ever been in. Going from floor to floor, I took my time examining furniture, pewter, copper, and brass, and even the small glass bottles which I found on the third floor.

The order in which everything had been arranged was as simple as it was ingenious. Cumbersome antiques, such as furniture, were placed on the ground floor; smaller things, on the second floor; and the smallest articles, such as old jewelry, on the top floor.

I thought this arrangement quite admirable. I realized, partly with pleasure and partly with chagrin, that there was hardly anything in this building I didn't want. After a while, I managed to narrow down my choice to a painted brandy flacon and a mirror with a glass frame.

The bottle, one the Stiegel type, so named after the German "Baron" Stiegel who established a glass factory in Pennsylvania in the 18th century, was very beautiful. Its traditional motif contained tulips and other flowers painted in white, red, and blue. The second firing contracted and raised the paint. In America, such work is referred to as

Stiegel *type* because no records of Stiegel's glass factory exist any longer. It is, therefore, impossible to claim that any particular bottle is a Stiegel product.

The frame of the mirror was an underglass painting. Yellow, orange and blue flowers were painted with great imagination and delicacy over, or rather—in this case—under the pale green background. It was a work of great beauty. Mr. Linares, the owner of this grandiose establishment, pointed out that this frame had been one of twelve which had hung in a covent and which showed the twelve apostles.

Underglass painting is always as rare as it is fragile; not much of it has survived the centuries. A primitive form of art practiced by village artisans, it is now virtually extinct.

The prices Mr. Linares wanted for bottle and mirror were high, yet if I were to sell them now, I could get six times what I paid. I hesitated; he was silent. In the end, I gave in and agreed to buy them. Having left my travellers checks in the hotel, I asked Mr. Linares to hold my purchases until the next day.

I liked Mr. Linares. He was obviously a cultivated man; and I would have dearly enjoyed talking to him about antiques, but I could see that he had to give his attention to other customers.

The shop was closing now; and I walked back to the hotel, warmed and happy in the thought that I had found two new treasures. I also made a decision. Having indulged myself by buying two high-priced antiques, I would go without dinner; and the best way to survive the evening was to go to bed very soon before I could give in to an understandable desire for a good meal.

The next morning I broke my self-imposed fast, and made my way—this time in an overcoat—to the antique shop. I paid my bill and made arrangements for the shipment. In the end I could not resist a desire to tell the amiable Mr. Linares how highly I had thought of his antiques and in what way I had disciplined myself for my extravagance. Mr. Linares shook his head. He was obviously dismayed. "Oh, Señor," he said, "you should not have done that. Señora Linares and I would have been so happy to have you as our guest for dinner." The way he said it I knew he meant it.

A few days later, I was in Seville. The weather was sunny and warm, and I watched a colorful procession march through the town. Little platforms with effigies of the Holy Virgin and the saints were held aloft. They were larger than life, and dressed in great splendor. After they passed, I visited a Moorish palace and the Archivo de las Indias. It is there that most documents of the Spanish colonies in the New World are kept. There was a letter written by Columbus to Queen Isabella. There were street plans of the big cities in South America, and for St. Augustine, Florida, the oldest town in North America.

During the hours of siesta, I walked through the medieval ghetto where alleyways separating the houses are hardly more than five feet wide. Turning a corner I saw that familiar name, "Linares," over a shop window. In contrast to the grand edifice in Madrid, this Linares store turned out to be a souvenir shop with just a few antiques. It was my impression that the owner might not always tell a customer what was new and what was old.

Among the few old things in this shop were some tiles,

decorated with flower designs in green, red and yellow. They were gaily painted.

Many houses in southern Spain have a border of tiles around their doors. Occasionally, one finds such tiles in antique shops. I thought that the eight which I had selected could be cemented on a wooden base and framed together in two rows of four.

When I talked to young Mr. Linares about it, he promised, cheerfully, to have such a frame made for me and to ship it when ready. "It will take two weeks, three weeks at the most," he assured me.

Three months after I returned home, long after I had received my beautiful bottle and mirror from Madrid and had given up all hope of ever getting the tiles, they finally arrived—just as I had picked them out from the counter, unassembled. The package contained no frame, just four separate pieces of molding.

When my letters to the nephew brought no results, I finally wrote the older Linares in Madrid; and at last I received an answer from Seville. "Señor Salter," it said, "Is not nice you make trouble for me with Uncle José. He is now angry with me. I sent you the tiles, no?"

Later, I had the frame made by a local mason, and took comfort in the fact that in Seville I had not missed dinner but had feasted on *gazpacho* and *paella* in the Hotel Alfonso XIII.

154

155

"The Bus—She Needs a Rest."

MALLORCA 1958

A poster near the bus stop at the Avenida Colon in Palma de Mallorca had promised, "a cool day at the refreshing beaches of Formentor!" So here I was on my way on a rickety old bus, and you'll never know what "rickety" is until you have been on an antique bus in Spain. We stopped in a small town. Here the passengers left the bus to eat something and to rest.

I suspect the bus needed a rest, too, from the rigors of travelling on stony roads and climbing hills. It was ancient like its driver, who spoke a little English.

"Señor," he said, "the bus she is human to me. We are friends. No? . . . She get tired. It is hot." I agreed with him.

The passengers had gone into a *bodega* for a glass of wine, and some *zarzuela*, a mixture of fish and seafood. I distrusted this dish on a hot day, and I ambled around the corner in the hope of finding a place where I could buy a sandwich.

The heat had made me drowsy. I stopped in front of a grocery store and looked at the fruit and vegetables in baskets and bins. I entered through a glass beaded curtain, and pointing to some green grapes, asked for half a pound. On a marble slab on the counter surrounded by buzzing flies lay a sweating salami. I took a chance and had the proprietress make me a sandwich. Armed with my lunch, I made my way back to the bus stop. When I arrived, still chewing but refreshed by the juicy grapes, I saw a cloud of dust disappearing around the corner. The bus had left without me. Presumably, she had had her rest.

I looked around for what might pass as a travel agency. There was none. All shops were closed. I sat down at the fountain in the market square, occasionally taking a sip of clear water, occasionally washing my hands or face. Finally, a friendly *viejo* limped along. He was dressed in a black suit, including a vest, and he wore a high-collared shirt and a hideous green flowered necktie. He seemed quite comfortable, despite the heat, and he was very friendly. I tried to explain my predicament in the little Spanish I knew.

He gestured elegantly, and to me his Spanish sounded magnificent. Eventually I understood that there would be no other bus that day going to Formentor, but that the bus I had been on would return around five o'clock. Now it was two, and siesta time.

The old man shrugged his shoulders. "The *tiendas* will be open at four o'clock, more or less," he added, vaguely. "It is cool there." I thanked him. The steps of the fountain were growing hotter, and I left them to explore the town.

I must have been walking for some time when I saw a sign which read *Antiquidades*. Hoping they would open soon, I peered through the dusty window at a man in the store. The man looked at me. Then he rose and came to the door and let me in.

The coolness of the shop was a great relief. The owner spoke French as many Mallorcans do. This was helpful. I tried to check with him the schedule of departing buses, but he merely shrugged his shoulders. I decided I had better watch the time.

At first impression, the shop did not seem very interesting; but since I had time, I searched patiently among over-decorated glasses and heavy bottles until I found something that pleased me. It was a small, crystal goblet on a silver base. The upper part of the glass was etched, de-

159

picting three demi-goddesses, generally known as "The Fates." The first holds the spindle or distaff, the second guides the thread through her hands, and the third holds shears ready to cut the thread at the appropriate time. Above "The Fates," the inscription reads in German, *"Spinnet noch lange!"* ("Spin on a long time!")

"How did this glass find its way to Mallorca?" I asked as I held it up to the light. The owner shrugged his shoulders, and quoted $15, a rather high price I thought; but the glass was unique, so I bought it without haggling.

I was about to leave when I noticed a small deck of cards. I looked at them, and was delighted. The freshness of their colors and the naive simplicity of the design made me feel that my afternoon in the town had not been wasted after all.

The four suits of the deck were swords—which I think may have been the forerunners of diamonds; cups—which are also found on Austrian and on Swiss cards; coins—which I have only seen on very old Italian or French cards; and clubs. But unlike our trefoil, these were actual clubs, certainly as lethal as swords. I learned later that I had bought a deck of *tarot* cards used by gypsies for fortune telling.

The cards were old, very old, and had been colored by hand. When I asked the price, the owner did not shrug his shoulders but let me have them for 300 *pesetas* ($5). Perhaps he knew I was in a hurry, and he did not want to lose the sale.

I walked rapidly toward the *Parada*. By running the last block and yelling "Stop! Stop!" as loud as I could, I was able to reach the bus before it turned the corner on its way back to Palma.

Museum Pieces All

AMSTERDAM 1961

Not far from the Amstelgracht, the Spiegelstraat cuts across the old town of Amsterdam. There is little traffic. I love this street because it has a generous sprinkling of antique shops.

Antique shops in Amsterdam are different from those in the towns and cities of France, Spain, or Italy. There is usually less haggling, and it is my impression that in these shops there are fewer restored pieces and outright forgeries. As everywhere else, one must be aware of articles obviously meant for the tourist trade. Too many antique shops depend on a quick sale, and unless you ask directly, you may not be told what is genuine and what has just come from a factory warehouse.

Space in the old part of Amsterdam is very limited; the houses seem pasted to each other on narrow cobblestone streets. You can still buy some beautiful old furniture here, as well as old copper and old brass: kettles, pans, pots, molds, all nicely shined.

And where but in Amsterdam can one find such a great selection of decorated tiles? These *tegels* are usually square, perhaps four by four inches—although some are oblong—and are most often decorated in what we have come to call Delft blue. Actually, this beautiful color came to Holland via the long overland route which Marco Polo took. The hue originated in China, and is produced by using small quantities of cobalt which turn into this unique blue color after firing. Some of these tiles are a purplish-mauve which was particularly popular in the 18th century, and some are painted in several colors, an effect not unlike Spanish or Italian Majolica.

For me, it has always been very hard to resist entering all these shops and buying something in each of them. That afternoon in September I had a ticket for a concert, and I was planning to leave the town early the next morning. After passing by two or three of the shops, I stopped in front of a small store which only showed tiles in the window. Prominently displayed was a picture made up of 48 tiles, arranged in six rows of eight. The composition depicted a Dutch man-of-war of the 17th century. I could judge the era from the flags on the ship and from the uniforms worn by the soldiers and sailors. The picture was framed in dark oak. Since all the other tiles displayed in the window were reasonably priced, I assumed that the painting I coveted was not for sale because it bore no price tag.

Inside the store stood several big tables. These were laden with tiles which rested in deep wooden trays. The proprietor pointed out to me that all the tiles on a certain table were priced at five guilders a piece, and those on another were priced at three guilders each. The tiles which were least expensive had been damaged.

165

Antique tiles can be easily recognized. In the first place, they do not carry any hallmarks. As a matter of fact, no Dutch tiles bore the name *Delft* until the tourists invaded Holland. Secondly, old tiles are not too uniform in size, though they seem to have been made approximately to the same measure. Thirdly, old tiles are rarely uniform in thickness. I have seen some which are fairly thin, and others which are quite thick. The surface of antique Dutch tiles is never smooth nor glossy as are tiles of modern manufactrue, but is quite uneven, probably due to the fact that freshly made tiles dry unevenly before they are glazed and fired. Most importantly, of course, is the distinctive method of decoration.

While a tile factory might have had orders for hundreds of conventional tulip or other flower designs, quite a few were made to order from designs submitted by individuals. Nothing was printed or stenciled; no decals were used; everything was painted free-hand. Some of these tiles were done by fine masters. The tiles shown on these pages might have been painted by a Rembrandt or perhaps copied from one of the Master's drawings or etchings.

But even a large production of many tiles of the same design would not turn out to be absolutely uniform. This is probably one of the reasons why we appreciate antiques so much, because we sense the sheer individuality of an artist who worked in an era when artifacts were not turned out by machines.

167

I had spent a good deal of time in this shop, and I bought a number of tiles, some of which I later had framed and which delight me to this day. The shopkeeper had given me much interesting information. The picture made up of tiles which I had admired in the window was much too expensive for me. I expressed my regret; and asked the owner if all he sold were individual tiles.

"Yes, for the most part," he answered. "But if you are interested in ceramics," he added with a little smile, "I can show you a nice collection." I said I was.

He conducted me up three flights of stairs to his attic. In the old houses of Amsterdam, steps are exceedingly steep. Sometimes, to ascend you have to hold onto a rope set at the side of the stairs. As I was climbing the unaccustomed steps, I had some misgivings, for looking at my wristwatch, I realized with concern that the hour of the concert was drawing near and I had not even had lunch. I knew it would have to be one or the other. But as things turned out, I was to give up both lunch and concert. For when I entered the attic room, so small and so nicely furnished, I found myself completely enchanted.

Spread out before me were magnificent examples of what seemed to be "Pennsylvania-Dutch" *slipware*. The pieces filled two corner cabinets, some tables, and even a vitrine. There were plain plates, and pie plates, and molds, and other articles of red clay, glazed and baked, and then painted in yellow, white and green, with decorative flowers and illustrations and with lettering characteristic of the 18th century. I must have gasped, for the shopkeeper was obviously satisfied with the effect the room had produced on me.

"How did you get all these wonderful pieces from Pennsylvania?" I naively exclaimed.

"They come from Limburg," he told me simply, pointing out a deep dish used for baking pies which was beautifully decorated with intricate tulip designs and an inscription. "It is Dutch, you see."

This was quite true, for the inscription was Dutch, and not German nor English as would have been the case on actual Pennsylvania-Dutch earthenware. He explained to me that the Swiss and Swabian immigrants who had traveled down the Rhine on rafts to Holland had temporarily settled in the vicinity of Limburg. Eventually, they had sailed for America and had landed in Philadelphia. They settled in Lancaster County where they were called the Dutch—later the Pennsylvania-Dutch. But it is likely that most of these people were of Swiss or German origin, farmers and woodsmen and not like the Dutch sailors and ship-builders, and that therefore, they should have been called Pennsylvania-Germans.

The next time I went to Holland, I profited from this new knowledge. I went directly to Limburg and looked for slipware. However, all I could find and afford was a charming little painted spoon rack which I have since used to hold my pewter spoons.

Everything in the little room in Amsterdam was exquisite, museum pieces all. When I asked my host if he had ever considered selling some of his treasures, he shook his head and told me that he had purchased each piece at personal sacrifice, and that he would not part with any of the collection even though he could not really afford to keep such a collection.

170

171

A Gift of Love

UPSALA 1961

There is not much one can do in a small Swedish town but to watch the swallows building their nests on the porch of the sleepy hotel or walk through the town park. Near the park stands a row of shops, one a *Konditorei*, in which every afternoon, people sit down and order coffee and cake.

One day in the Konditorei, I made the acquaintance of the daughter of the proprietor. She was a beautiful blonde with a dimpled smile, and could hardly have been older than four. The waitress, who spoke a little English, called her the daughter of the "bakerman." While I was sitting at the round marble-topped table drinking my coffee, the child gravely walked through the Konditorei, turning here and there. Finally stopping in front of me, she made a deep curtsy. Since I did not speak Swedish, all I could do was to bow just as gravely. This made her laugh, and she ran back behind the counter where her mother, busy with cakes, talked to her in chiding tones. Since the mother knew no English, our conversation was limited to gestures, such as pointing to some pieces of cake.

The next time I saw little Ingeborg, she was seated at one of the tables with a coloring book and some crayons. As the time for my departure neared, I decided to give her a small gift. In a nearby stationery shop I found what I wanted—a little set of colored pencils, complete with a shiny pencil sharpener.

When I came back to the Konditorei, I learned, with

the help of the waitress, that the child had been sent to bed early because she had been naughty. I asked the waitress to tell the mother that I wanted to give the child a little farewell gift. After some discussion, Ingeborg was brought in, a little red robe over her nightgown. She had been crying, but she smiled when she saw me, and her eyes widened with pleasure when the little box was presented to her. She ran into the back room, but she returned immediately, now quite oblivious of her punishment. She was carrying some paper, and she sat herself down at my table and began to draw a picture.

Her mother was obviously pleased and displeased at the same time. She talked earnestly with her daughter, and the interpreter informed me that little Ingeborg's punishment was not over and she would have to go back to bed. Back she went . . . I was sorry to see her go. But a few minutes later, just as I was ready to leave, she came in once more, stepping cautiously on tiptoes, hoping her mother would not see her. In her hand she held a little wooden rooster, a traditional Swedish toy, painted in colorful hues similar to the primitive wooden articles found in Austria and Switzerland.

Like those two Alpine countries, northern Scandinavia is rich in woodlands; and the natives like to whittle and carve during the long, cold winters. Like all primitive European woodwork, colorful paints are applied in bold designs. In Austria, much of this work is of a religious nature; in Sweden and Norway, the wood carvers tend toward the making of toys. Roosters, and horses of an orange color have always been among the most popular Swedish toys. Wherever wood is cut into boards and made into furniture and into small useful articles, decorations are applied. The most popular of all motifs seems to be the tulip, perhaps because this flower abounds in so many colors. In cases where it is not practical to paint the wood (for example, a kitchen spoon) decorative designs are carved into the wood.

Ingeborg pressed the little toy rooster in my hand, all the while earnestly talking to me, confident that I would understand her. All I could do was to smile at her.

At last her mother came around from behind the counter and the interpreter said to me, "The little girl says, sir, that she wants you to have a toy, too, so you don't have to sit alone when you drink coffee and eat cake."

Today, Ingeborg must be a pretty sixteen-year-old girl, wearing the Swedish student's cap. Her little rooster still keeps me company on my breakfast table.

The next day, a fast train took me past glittering lakes and through green forests to Stockholm. My destination was Upsala, the medieval university town where I planned to see one of the oldest and most beautiful manuscript Bibles in existence, the *codex argenteus*. The text, applied in silver uncial letters to parchment dyed a beautiful deep pink, is a translation of the New Testament. From the Greek of the Evangelists, Bishop Ulfila fashioned a translation into sixth-century Latin. This Bible is surely the most magnificent I have ever seen.

When I came away from seeing the *codex argenteus*, I felt overcome by so much beauty. What I had seen bridged fourteen centuries; and here I was walking in the streets of an old Swedish university town, hearing foreign sounds but viewing contemporary buildings, people, and vehicles.

After a while, I woke up from my entrancement, when I was almost run over by a speeding car, driving on what seemed to me to be the wrong side of the road. I stopped in front of a restaurant called *Strandkelleren*. To the right of it, there was a prosaic haberdashery store; and to its left, an antique shop!

When going to antique shops becomes an important activity in one's life, you get to know not only what the stores look like and how they are organized, but also how antiques are priced. Sometimes pieces are openly priced and bear a sticker or a tag. More commonly the price is not revealed. But more important than acquiring knowledge about authenticity, styles, value, etc., is that the antique hunter becomes acquainted with men and women who share his love for fine old things. Some of these store owners know their stuff, others don't. It is a gratifying experience when you go into an antique shop and meet an attractive, friendly person who will put you at your ease, and with whom you can share knowledge—yours and his.

Mrs. Lindquist—her name was on the business card which I picked up from a silver tray—was such a person. She showed me what she had to offer, and she volunteered interesting facts about those articles which had attracted my attention.

There were a few pressed glass, cup-shaped lanterns in shades of ruby, sapphire, and amethyst. These might be hung on Christmas trees with burning candles inside of them to give off a lovely light, or they could be placed on

a windowsill to illuminate the house on special occasions. This made me think of something. "Is it true," I asked, "that on Christmas morning Swedish girls serve breakfast to their families while wearing headdresses fitted with burning candles?"

"Well, not exactly," answered Mrs. Lindquist. "It is on the thirteenth of December, Santa Lucia Day, when we commemorate the martyred saint who was blinded by soldiers. On this day, the oldest girl in the family, or the mother, will wear a wreath of *lingonberries*, and on it there will be burning candles. It is a lovely custom," she said, smilingly, "but it is not on Christmas day."

During the course of an hour or so, I selected a wooden tray with some broad-bladed stag knives and some two-pronged forks, a half a dozen of each utensil.

"These come from a hunting lodge near Stockholm," said Mrs. Lindquist. "The owner replaced everything with stainless steel! So we have these here now."

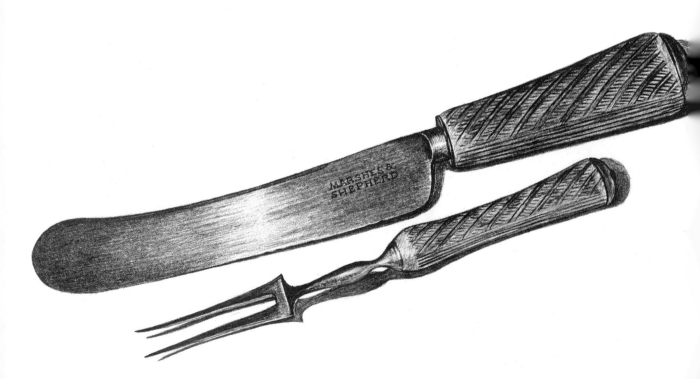

"And what do we do for spoons?" I asked, jokingly. Mrs. Lindquist had an answer.

She handed me a two-piece bronze mold in which there was a pewter spoon which fitted in the mold quite naturally, since it had been cast from it.

"There is only one spoon left," she said, regretfully, "but you can cast many more, I'm sure. People in those days melted and re-cast utensils whenever their spoons were battered or bent. You can do the same. All you need is some old pewter."

The spoons we cast from the mold became dearer to us than our silver. To this day we eat cereals, soups, and stews with our pewter spoons, cast from a Swedish spoon mold.

"In the Name of His Majesty, the King"

MUNICH 1965

Each day, just a few minutes before noon, people crowd into the Town Hall Square in Munich. Traffic comes to a standstill. The reason: a spectacle which has attracted the people of Munich for centuries, and of course, all those who visit this beautiful city.

There is a great clock on the bell tower of the Town Hall. The crowd gathers to watch the big hand advance. When it reaches 12, two giant metal figures ponderously hammer out 12 resounding blows against an enormous bronze bell. The people are attentive and silent. As the sound dies away, other beautifully painted figures come to life. Drummers drum. Trumpeters lift trumpets to their lips. Knights and their ladies bow to each other in courtly manner. The figures move around the tower several times, then stop dead just where they are, to wait for another day. The Square returns to normal: to the hustle and bustle of slow-moving traffic, and the sight of impatient pedestrians.

Once, when I stood marvelling in front of this wondrous clock, a sudden heavy shower surprised the watchers. Only the very hardy stood fast; the rest of us pushed back to huddle in dryer places. Somehow I found myself propelled into a small shop.

In this particular location, this sort of thing happens often enough so that the shop owners take it philosophically. They do not expect a sale to develop.

Looking around the store, I noticed some rather ugly

modern steins. A young salesgirl offered to assist me. I inquired in German if those were the only steins. She hesitated, and then began to praise those horrors, quoting prices, and then pointed out some other articles. Although German is my mother tongue, she must have sensed that I was a foreign tourist. Most items displayed were obviously for the tourist trade. I looked at her for a moment and said in my best Bavarian, "Those, I don't care for."

She answered my look with an impish smile. "If the gentleman will wait a moment...."

She disappeared for several minutes, leaving me under the watchful eye of the shopkeeper, who had hitherto remained silent at his desk in the rear of the shop. It is typical of the mentality of small shopkeepers to let their helpers earn their bread. This man was no exception. He had watched to see how the girl would manage. If he had felt that the sale was not going well, he would undoubtedly have interfered.

183

Presently the girl returned, holding in each hand a magnificent antique stein. She placed them before me on the table.

"There now!" I said. "That's more like it."

At this point the previously indifferent owner sprang into action. He came over, all servility.

"This," he said, "is a very fine specimen of *Biedermeier*. And this one is a late 17th-century piece. If you will note the hallmark in the pewter."

I cut him short.

"The young lady was just telling me about them," I lied firmly. The shopkeeper tightened his mouth and withdrew.

I was rewarded with a grateful smile which I have not forgotten through the years. Anyway, the steins are in my living room to remind me.

I was in a buying mood that day. The steins had cost $12 each and they were museum pieces. I took them safely

185

to my hotel and left immediately with a feeling of certainty that I should buy at least one more antique that day. I had earlier seen a little porcelain plaque hanging on the wall of a shop window. On it in bold, blue letters in old-fashioned German was the plea for "daily bread" from The Lord's Prayer. From the spelling I concluded that the plaque was at least 150 years old. The shop, situated in the Prinzregentenstrasse not far from the Hotel Vier Jahreszeiten, specialized in antique kitchen implements. I looked them over carefully but found nothing I wanted except the plaque. Then the owner, a short stocky man dressed very much like a Bavarian peasant, drew my attention to a draft notice dated 1810. It was the oldest draft notice I had ever seen.

This order was issued to a young Bavarian and began, rather pompously: "In the Name of His Majesty the King . . ." The request to report for duty was couched in considerably stronger terms than the plea for daily bread, and I considered this noteworthy.

My visit to Munich was a success. When I later visited the Landeskunst Museum, I had the pleasure of viewing one of the finest collections of primitive folk art I've ever seen. Objects made of pewter, copper, brass and silver, glasses and painted bottles, filled the showcases. Painted wardrobes and chests, carved chairs and benches, bedsteads and wall panelling, hundreds of under-glass paintings constituted a wondrous collection. I've only one under-glass painting, and indeed I deem it very precious.

8441 N.23.

Praes: d 11 Mai 1810.

Bamberg
am 5. May
1810.

Im Namen
Seiner Majestät des Königs

Das Rübreactorat zu Scheinfurt erhält hier die Abschrift eine allerhöchsten bestätigte genauen Begleitung, und zu gütlichem Vorschlägen ergehen lassen, sobald der Mühe noch die herzmächtigste sein möge.

General Commissariat des Mainkreises

(Unterschrift)

Als die Abschrift im Census-Buche.
zu suchen noch einmal unter No 25 b.)

(Unterschrift)

An
das Rübreactorat zu
Scheinfurt
Scheinfurt Neheimen betr.

Just Like the Old Kaiser Franz Josef

SALZBURG 1965

Salzburg, its history, surroundings, and musical life, is synonymous with Mozart, and in our time, with the *Salzburger Festspiele*.

I have spent many happy weeks at the nearby St. Wolfgangsee in the Villa Nebrich, a small, private hotel decorated with many antiques and run by its charming owner, Mrs. Doris Renner. I have visited Gmunden at the Traunsee, an old Austrian resort where my parents took me when I was five; Schloss Fuschl, an 18th-century baroque hunting lodge; and I even have had coffee and cake at the Cafe Zauner in Bad Ischl, just like old Kaiser Franz Josef did.

Sometimes the weather was good; often it rained for days, as is expected in the Salzkammergut. I spent such days in museums, castles, and in the magnificent baroque churches of Salzburg, and in the countryside; and of course, I went to antique shops.

A trip to the resort of Gmunden brought me two lovely baroque pewter pieces. Both were coffeepots, but one was intended for mocha. Fluted like most baroque pieces are, their covers were hinged on the side—not at the back—which prevented spilling the liquid. They were classic in their beauty; and for that reason did not seem too expensive at about $20 apiece.

Because it rained, I stayed longer and at last bought a

large candlestick, two feet high, made of pewter which could be disassembled into three pieces. This was not a candle-holder but a candlestick. A "candlestick" has a spike on which a candle (usually a big candle) is stuck. Such large candlesticks were used at the sides of altars, and next to coffins during funeral services.

In Salzburg in the Getreidegasse near Mozart's house, I found a shop which had only a few antiques. A young, friendly girl, dressed in a dirndl, waited on me. I bought a hand-colored print of Austrian soldiers of the period of the Napoleonic wars. The uniforms of the time were like the dress uniforms of today, colorful if not practical. Field gray and olive drab uniforms were not yet in use.

For about $5 I also bought a square textile-printing block which was made up of innumerable tiny brass nails,

193

used for printing cotton fabric for dirndls. Such blocks are dipped in a thick substance, which is used to print on the cloth. After the substance hardens, the cloth is usually dyed a dark blue. When the dye has set, the thick substance is boiled out, leaving white dots and other shapes on the blue background. Cloth for dirndls is still being made—probably by large presses—but the charm of my old printing block still remains.

In this shop, there were also a few old *Spanschächtel-chen*. These are small oval boxes, made out of wood that has been split so thin it becomes flexible when wet and so can be curved and made into boxes. These little containers, used for many purposes, ranged in size from two inches to two feet. Sometimes they were round; more often they were oval or were rectangular with rounded corners. They were charmingly decorated in colorful floral designs, and I was happy to get them. And I'm still very pleased today to have them. These boxes are very delicate. Contemporary ones, made in the old tradition by contemporary artisans, are equally attractive and make ideal souvenirs and gifts. They can be purchased to this day at the *Tyroler Heimatwerk* in Salzburg for approximately a dollar apiece.

It was in this shop, too, that we found a pair of baroque candle holders which matched our coffeepots and our pitcher. The word *matching,* as used here, must not be taken too literally. Since artifacts have always been made

by individual artisans who followed the style of the day as a matter of course, variations were produced and still are. To my way of thinking, there is more charm in such articles when you *feel* they match, than if they came in identical patterns from a mail-order house.

After our little purchase, we decided to call it a day, and motored back to St. Gilgen where an excellent dinner of *tafelspitz* and *Salzburger nockerln* awaited us.

Whatever it is that brings you to Salzburg—be it the opera, the concerts, the scenery, or the antique shops—Salzburg is always a happy experience. This charming town is one to remember, and one to look forward to. It has never failed to give me a lift.

Route Seven and Northern Boulevard

CONNECTICUT AND LONG ISLAND 1969

"We'll come, if you'll let Bob watch the World Series."

This was an answer to our invitation to our friends, Bob and Marge, to spend a long weekend with us in Connecticut. He liked baseball. She loved antique hunting.

They arrived on Saturday morning. In the afternoon, Bob excused himself to watch the game. Marge told us that on the way out to us from Long Island they had passed a fabulous antique shop on Northern Boulevard. Bob had not wanted to stop because he didn't want to miss the first inning. That evening, sitting around the barbecue, when the smoke was getting into our eyes and the mosquitoes under our skin, and with the delicious aroma of thick charcoal broiled sirloin filling the air, Marge said to Bob, "Tomorrow morning, we'd like to drive to Route 7 to see the beautiful foliage and maybe visit an antique shop or two; but we'll be back in time for you to see the game."

Bob looked worried. "I want to be sure of that," he said. "It's a very important game." Then he magnanimously added, "I might be willing to hear an inning or two on the radio."

The next morning, after a hearty country breakfast, we took off in the direction of Danbury. In those days, Route 7 was a haven for antique hunters because there were a great many antique shops between the Merritt Parkway and Danbury. There still are today.

Interesting antiques eluded us that morning. Prices were

higher than we had thought they would be, and the shops were pretty crowded. Bob had refused to come along into the shops, and sat in the car reading a book. From time to time he looked at his watch.

However, near Wilton we found a table, surprisingly inexpensive at $15. We had the feeling that it must have quietly survived, generation after generation, tucked away in some cozy corner of a pre-Victorian home. Made of curly maple, it presented a curious, almost puzzling effect. Under the tabletop, there was one large drawer which followed the curved contour of the front. It would be hard to describe the curious pedestal of four legs coming out of a thick center post. But the table looked comfortable—it still is—though it turned out to be a curious mixture of styles.

It was only when we returned home that we discovered that the top of this table had once rested on four slender legs. They must have been damaged beyond repair, and could not be replaced. The pedestal had undoubtedly been the underpinning of some other table, probably a round one. One may safely assume that the pedestal had, in some manner, lost its top and that it had been mated with a legless top. It is truly a mutt; but like all mutts, friendly and comfortable.

We turned back along Route 7. Just before the Parkway, we came to another store which seemed to feature bottles and pressed glass. We wanted some colorful bottles for the windows on either side of our front door.

Many of the bottles were reproductions. This was not difficult to determine because they neither had *pontil* marks

201

nor did the glass seem to be the kind commonly used during the 19th century. There is a certain charm in the unevenness of glass with irregular bubbles, and in other such manifestations of a living glass-blower's hands and lungs. What a contrast from the indifference of a glass-blowing machine.

We found a whole bin of old ink bottles commonly used in schools and post offices around the time of the Civil War. They came in many colors—brown, blue, green, and clear. We took one of each color. It is interesting to note that austerity in design and production often makes finer

shapes than the overly decorated pieces so common at the turn of the century.

We stopped for cokes and hamburgers; and then we were rushed off by Bob who was eager to get back to his television set to watch the rest of the World Series game.

Just two blocks from our house, we noticed a sale that was going on. We left the car, and Bob went on home by himself. The tag sale had obviously been going on all morning and it did not look promising; but there is always something you can buy at a tag sale, be it a chest of drawers good enough for a child's room or a diminutive roasting pan. I consented to go along, provided that my wife would refrain from buying broken-down bridge tables or some odd tablecloths too small to be useful. Some neighbors were sitting on the lawn, the children drinking cokes and eating cookies. A miniature poodle, tied to a tree, was yipping at all newcomers indiscriminately.

It took but a few glances to see there was very little that we wanted. However, in a corner of the garage there were two kitchen chairs that looked to me like Windsor chairs. They were painted white with blue trim. These had not been tagged. I could tell that they might prove attractive if two or three layers of paint were removed and the chairs sanded down and refinished; but I also knew I wasn't going to do the job. The matter was decided for me when the woman running the sale told my wife that we could have both chairs for $4, since they were kind of rickety.

When I was assured that I would not have to help with the refinishing but that a cabinet maker would do the job for very little—very little turned out to be $15 apiece—I put both chairs over my shoulders; and we walked home Indian file.

204

"How did you make out?" asked Bob when we returned.

"Fine," we told him.

"How about you?"

He sneered. "My team was ahead by three runs—but it isn't anymore."

When our friends were ready to go home the next day, we followed them in our station wagon to the "fabulous" antique shop on Northern Boulevard. Again Bob stayed outside reading. His team had lost the World Series.

Yes, here was the antique shop everybody dreams about. There was furniture; there were bottles; there was pewter;

there was copper; there was antique jewelry. All of it was interesting, and most of it was good.

A multi-colored perfume bottle standing in a charming Baroque vitrine attracted our attention. It was quite different from most of the colored glass I had ever seen. Innumerable fragments of many colors—including tiny silver flecks—floated in the glass. This indicated to me that small remnants of colored glass had been incorporated into some clear glass, and had, in the process of being blown, blended into the clear glass. After the small bottle had been blown, the glass-blower pressed both sides of the piece on metal to flatten the bottle. When the bottle cooled, a pattern had been cut into it with great skill. A fine perfume flacon had come to life. I let the sun shine through the precious little thing and enjoyed its beauty. It is probably the most unusual bottle in our collection.

Then we noticed a pale green three-mold bottle much like a blue one we had bought in Virginia some years earlier. As we were wondering whether we could afford to buy both or only one, Marge settled the problem by insisting on giving us the perfume bottle as a gift.

For herself, Marge found a garnet bracelet. She also discovered a set of four painted egg cups which she planned to use for little plants.

After a while, we saw an old copper mold made in the shape of a curved fish. The dealer assured us that it had originally come from the estate of Theodore Roosevelt. That little bit of information, of course, brought up the price, but when I pointed out that the mold was in need of cleaning and re-tinning, the price went down to where it should have been in the first place. "Sold!" I said.

207

Marge and Bob left for home. We went on looking. As we were beginning to tire, we both noticed an interesting piece of furniture in a corner. It was a dry sink, unusual in that it had a superstructure with drawers for knives and forks and a shelf for cups and glasses. We thought it might be used as a small bar to house bottles, glasses, and the like. The sink or bar—we have called it by both names for a long time now—was in good shape. Like all old furniture, it could be tightened up and refinished, but it could also be used as is. I see the sense of removing several layers of unattractive paint to unveil the beautiful wood of a Windsor chair, but I do not think that every piece of furniture you own must be in mint condition.

We paid the asking price of $32, and carted off the sink in our station wagon.

It had been a great weekend.

209

The Left Bank and the Right Bank

of the River Seine

PARIS 1970

When we arrived in Paris on the third of September at 7 A.M., we had no hotel reservations. The American tourists hadn't left Paris as yet, and the French tourists from the provinces had invaded the city to attend the great event of the year, the annual automobile show, *Le Salon*.

After many weeks of living in grand hotels, in small, quaint inns, in charming pensions, and in clean tourist accommodations overlooking ice-covered mountains, we finally met our nemesis.

A taxi had taken us all of two blocks to the Hotel la F. The tourist information office at the Gare de l'Est had supplied us with the name of the only hotel which had an available room.

We sized up the situation. Here was the *patron* dressed in pajamas and an old bathrobe, half-asleep. Here was the maid, the telephone operator, and the cook—his wife—barefoot and untidy. Here was the hotel, sleezy and musty, showing traces of former elegance, a faded antique.

Our room wasn't ready, so we left our luggage with some misgivings and walked down and explored the neighborhood. A few blocks from the hotel we breakfasted in a bakeshop on chocolate and freshly baked rolls with sweet butter and Gruyère. Then we wandered back to the hotel.

Searching further for a better place in Paris seemed useless—quite useless, it turned out—when dozens of telephone calls, even to the most expensive hotels, yielded no results.

Our room was just like the people who ran the hotel. It is amusing to think about it now, half a year later, but quite dismal when it was the only shelter we could find. During our short stay in Paris, we left the Hotel la F. the moment we were dressed in the morning, and returned in the evenings only when we were exhausted.

We had a tight program during our stay, going to the Louvre several times, walking up and down the Champs Elysées and experiencing Paris in sun and in rain. We saw what all tourists come to see, but we also braved the interminable steps of the Métro and explored its intricate underground passages.

We ate well in Paris. At the Café de la Paix we were served thirty delicious hors d'oeuvres from a rotating table; at Pruniers we partook of rich seafoods, and a great *bouillabaisse*; and at the home of an old friend, we were treated to a *mousse au chocolat*.

One morning, we wandered across the Ile de la Cité to the Left Bank, and to the many bookstalls lining the Seine. Everyone seemed to be browsing aimlessly. We decided to concentrate on one or two of the more promising stands.

The bookstalls at the Seine are a pleasure. Sooner or later, you find just about anything you might be looking for. Surprises await. Ours came in the form of a slender, pale blue booklet. When we opened its accordian-folded pages, they turned out to form a single illustration. Twenty-six French soldiers were grouped in alphabetical order from adjutant to *zouave*. There were fuseliers and grenadiers and even a *vivandière*—a camp follower. They were all clad in the dark blue coats of the army of Napoleon III, the soldiers in their famous red trousers, the vivandière in red pantaloons beneath her skirt. The buttons, the sabers, and the captions were printed in gold. This magnificent alphabet, one of several in a series, was printed long ago on lithographic stones, perhaps to help young schoolboys learn their ABCs and become acquainted with the uniforms of the *Grande Armée*.

I measured the page size with my fingers and estimated the alphabet to be six inches in height and—six feet in length!

When I was a child I owned a wooden box filled with just such soldiers, half of them Prussians, half of them French, all in the very same uniforms as this alphabet book.

The dealer, an aged man, dressed in an old overcoat, bent over towards us. He peered at us through thick lenses. "I won't let you have this book for less than twelve *nouveaux francs*," he croaked. We agreed hastily, and left before he could change his mind.

We spent the next day with our friends in St. Germain. Paulette, and her son, Julien, who knew our enthusiasm for antiques, suggested that we attend an auction which was taking place that evening.

The auction was half over when we arrived; but toward the end, a basket filled with battered copper molds and pots and pans was offered. These had come from the kitchen of an old hotel which had been torn down to make room for a new expressway. The bidders, who had probably come in the hope of finding appliances and furniture, were not interested in old copper.

A man sitting next to us exclaimed, "*Que voulez vous?* It is old copper, no? We need plastic and aluminum. It

213

A a B b C c

| Adjudant | Bonnet-Chinois Chinese Bonnet | Commandant Major |

214

D d

Dragon
Dragoon

cleans better!'' And so, to the amusement of the audience, we bid on a dozen beautiful copper molds, a large copper roasting pan, and some copper pots with covers, all for $65. They thought the foolish Americans had been robbed.

215

I have always been interested in copper molds, and I could tell that these were old ones made from heavy copper sheets, the pots and pans reinforced with brass. The many reproductions one sees today are made of much flimsier material and molded in less intricate shapes. The copper pieces sold at the auction had surely been stored in some obscure corner for many years and had become tarnished and dented. The tin lining had deteriorated. When we came home, it took a little searching to find a metal shop able to restore our copper pieces. We made a deal. We turned over some of our wares to the shop owner in exchange for clean-

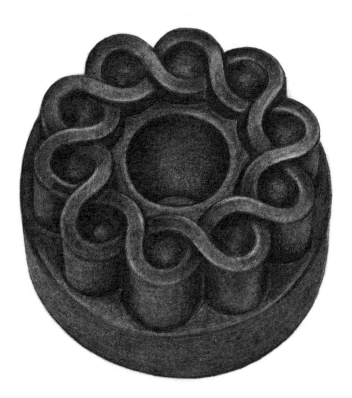

ing the copper thoroughly with acids and steel brushes. He gave the insides of all the pieces a new coating of tin, and polished the outsides to their original brilliance.

When we left Paris and our friends, we promised to return—but not to the Hotel la F.

217

The Glossary

ALBERTINA   Museum in Vienna founded by Prince Albert of Saxony, housing an unusual collection of musical manuscripts, many by Mozart and Haydn. There are also paintings, including the famous *Rabbit* watercolor by Albrecht Dürer. The museum also has an auditorium where concerts are presented.

ALDUS   In full, Aldus Manutius, but better known as Aldus. He was one of the early Italian printers and scholars who brought to the Italian scholastic world the classics of Greece and Rome. Aldus was the originator of a style of *Italic* type, which simulated the elegant penmanship of the Renaissance scribes. Queen Elizabeth the I of England was one of the finest of these. Aldine editions are rare and much sought after.

ALSTADT   (German, "old town") The original section of a town. Most European cities have such a section in contrast to the newer part of the city, sometimes called *Neustadt* or "New Town."

AMSTELGRACHT   One of the beautiful major *grachts* (canals) of Amsterdam. This canal was named for the Amstel River, from which the city itself derived its name.

AMSTERDAM   Capital of The Netherlands, often called the "Venice of the North" because of the several concentric canals that encircle the city. The old section of Amsterdam has not changed its character during the last three hundred years. Amsterdam is a world center of the diamond industry, and its colorfulness has made it a favorite of tourists.

ANTIK REGI, ANTIQUIDADES, ANTIQUITATEN   Hungarian, Spanish and German for Antique Shop.

ANTIQUARIAT   A book store specializing in rare or first editions. Also, a sale center for second-hand books, usually situated near colleges and schools.

ARCHIVO DE LAS INDIAS   A combined archive, museum, and library in Seville, Spain. It houses an untold wealth of documents, materials, and art of the Spanish colonies in the New World, as well as material pertaining to the present-day republics of South and Central America, and material from Mexico, Old California, Arizona, New Mexico, and Florida. All lands originally colonized by the Kingdom of Spain, from the West Indies to the Philippines, are represented here, a glorious array of the history of four centuries, from 1492 to 1899. This is one of the most interesting archives in Europe.

ARNO   The river flowing through Florence. Spanned by several bridges, it includes the famous Ponte Vecchio, with its many interesting shops.

ASCONA   A mountainous Swiss town in the Italian-speaking Canton of Ticino or Tessin. At one time, it was part of Italy.

AUF WIEDERSEHEN   (German, "Until we see each other again") Goodbye.

AVENIDA COLON   (Spanish, "Avenue [Christopher] of Columbus") A popular street name in Spain.

BACCARAT   Famous French glass of the mid-nineteenth century.

BAD ISCHL   An Austrian mountain spa, one of the many *Bäder* (plural of *bad* meaning "bath"). Bad Ischl was made famous by the yearly sojourn of the Austrian Emperor Franz Josef, also because of its proximity to the St. Wolfgang See and the well-known White Horse Inn.

BAHNHOFSTRASSE   (German, "railroad street") There is usually one such thoroughfare in every German-speaking town.

BAROQUE   Around 1700, an Italian architect by the name of Barocco became popular as a builder of palaces. According to Lernet-Holenia, an Austrian historian, Baroque owes its name to this architect. Fundamentally, a departure from the classicism of the Renaissance. Baroque architecture, which had its greatest flowering in the churches of Europe, utilized unusual curves and irregularly shaped walls. The period lasted for two centuries, from the mid-sixteenth to the mid-eighteenth. The Baroque style was followed by a newer, daintier, more playful form, called the Rococo.

BATH   A town in Somerset, England, known for its beautiful, pure Regency architecture.

BEACON HILL   One of Boston's best-known, quietly elegant streets. It is situated opposite The Common, and the State House (Capitol) is at the top of the hill.

BIEDERMEIER   (German, "good citizen.") The Empire style in German-speaking countries. In England, this style corresponds to Regency.

BITTE   (German. "Please;" also "welcome.")

"BLACK ART"   Epithet given to Johann Gutenberg's invention of printing in the mid-fifteenth century. The reference is to the seemingly magical speed with which pages were reproduced, a task that formerly took a scribe hours of tedious manual work to complete.

BODEGA   (Spanish) A small wineshop and restaurant.

BOOK OF HOURS   A book of prayers and devotions for the entire year. These were hand-lettered and illustrated at great cost for royalty and the affluent.

BOSCH, HIERONYMOUS   Dutch painter of the fifteenth century. This artist of the Northern Renaissance was known for his fantastic and weird interpretations of hell. A realistic, satirical painter of tremendous imagination, he is represented in all major museums.

BOUILLABAISSE   The famous fish soup of Marseilles, France, served wherever there are patriotic chefs and wooden tables, particularly on the Cannebière, a harbor street in Marseilles. This internationally famous dish is never the same twice, because the cook must depend on what variety of fish is available.

BRENNER PASS   A mountain pass leading from Austria's Tyrol to Italy's Alto Adige (upper Etsch, Tyrol's main river). The main artery of traffic between Germany, Austria, and Italy, it is of great strategic importance.

BRUEGHEL, PIETER   One of the best-known Flemish painters of the Northern Renaissance. Brueghel is known for his rural scenes, which reproduce faithfully and in great detail life in the Flemish region between France and Holland. Clothing and articles are depicted exactly as used by peasants, burghers, and soldiers. Among his famous biblical paintings is the *Slaughter of the Innocents* which now hangs in the Brussels Museum.

BROADSIDE   A poster of the 18th and 19th centuries, the forerunner of many types of popular printed matter such as sheet music, comic strips, and picture books.

BROMPTON ROAD   A shopping street in London's West End. Harrod's department store, small teahouses, colorful antique shops, and many boutiques are located here.

BRUGES   A Flemish town. "Brügge" in Flemish. Another "Venice of the North," but smaller than Amsterdam. Virtually unchanged since the Medieval Period. The town contains a small, very fine museum with examples of the art of the work of Hieronymous Bosch, Pieter Breughel, Rogier van der Weyden, and Gerard David. Brügge has beautiful churches, and an interesting cobblestone market-square, and is within a few miles of Belgium's famous bathing resort, Ostende.

BUNKER HILL   Near Boston, Massachusetts, this is an historic site of the first significant encounter between the British Troops and the American Colonists.

CAFÉ MÜNCHEN   A small café. One of thousands in central Europe, destroyed during World War II.

CAFÉ DE LA PAIX   A landmark in Paris at the Place de l'Opèra and the Boulevard des Italiens. Famous for its excellent food and, in particular, for its great ferris wheel of varied hors d'ouevres.

CAFÉ ZAUNER   A small café in Bad Ischl, made famous by visits of the Austrian Emperor Franz Josef who knew good pastry when he tasted it. The café serves Austrian pastry at its very best, surpassed only by that of Dehmel in Vienna.

CAMPANILE   The bell tower of every Italian church. The best known campanile is in Florence, designed and built by the famous Italian painter and architect, Giotto. Next to this campanile is the Baptistry with its door made of bronze panels by Lorenzo Ghiberti. Endangered by the great flood of Florence in 1966, this great work of art was rescued and restored.

CANALE GRANDE   The main waterway of Venice, circling the original city with its many little canals. It is open to gondolas, motorboats, and small steamers called *vaporetti*.

CANTON TICINO   One of Switzerland's 22 states or provinces, most of them almost 700 years old. Each one is extremely loyal, no visible borders, and is subject only to the laws of the Federal Republic of Switzerland, the oldest republic in the world. The language of most cantons is German; some, French; of a very few, Italian; and of only one Romansch, a form of Latin.

CASA SERODINE   A patrician residence in Ascona, Switzerland, built in the 17th century. Now housing an antique shop, it is a fine example of Baroque architecture.

CASIMIR'S PEWTER SHOP   A unique antique shop on Brompton Road, London, specializing exclusively in the finest English pewter.

CHAMPS ELYSÉES   (French, "Elysian Fields.") The avenue of avenues, planned and built by Baron Hausmann in the Paris of post-revolutionary and Napoleonic days. Lined with the finest shops, restaurants, and hotels. The avenue leads from the Place de la Concorde to the Arc de Triomphe.

CHARGER   A large, round pewter serving plate.

CHARLOTTENBURG   The western section of Berlin, named for the castle built by a Prussian king for his wife, Charlotte.

CHIPPENDALE, THOMAS   The most famous English cabinetmaker of the 18th Century.

CODEX ARGENTEUS   (Latin "Silver Book") A manuscript Bible of purple-stained parchment leaves, lettered in silver throughout, the most famous Bible before the advent of printing. Probably commissioned by the Gothic missionary, Ulfila, and completed during the Fifth or the Sixth Century, it eventually found its way to the University of Upsala in Sweden.

COMMON   In Boston, as in many New England towns and villages, the Common is a square piece of land where townsmen and villagers once kept their cattle on a common grazing ground. The Boston Common is now a park.

CONDOTTIERE COLLEONI   (Italian, "leader" or "general.") Colleoni was one of the many Italian generals of the Renaissance period commissioned by governments of cities such as Venice, Florence, and Pisa, to wage war upon each other.

CONFITURE   (French, "confectionery" or "something made with sugar") In France, Belgium and all of Switzerland, *confiture* is used in place of the word "jam."

COVENT GARDEN (Probably derived from "convent garden") A small section of London next to Haymarket, in which London's large wholesale food market is situated. The famous London opera house is called Covent Garden.

CRUMPET Crumpets and scones are inevitably served with tea in England. Presumably the same is true for English colonies. Crumpets are akin to English muffins.

DAVID, GERARD Flemish painter. See Brügge.

DECILITRE One-tenth of a litre which rougly equals a quart in liquid measure.

DELFT Old, handsome Dutch town, famous for an adaptation of Chinese pottery. Delft is the characteristic blue color of this pottery, a shade between cobalt and Prussian blue. Delft is also the birthplace of the great Dutch painter, Jan Vermeer.

DOUBLE-DECKER BUS A type of bus still in use in London, resembling the Fifth Avenue coaches of yesteryear. Romantic in the summer, they are cold and clammy when it rains.

DUOMO (Italian "dome" or "house of God.")

DUPONT COLLECTION (Winterthur, Delaware) A comprehensive collection of American furniture, household articles, and artifacts dating from the mid-sixteenth century to the end of the Victorian era.

EL GRECO Greek painter who lived in Toledo, Spain, during the 16th Century. His name was Domenico Teotocopulo, but he was called El Greco or "The Greek" by his contemporaries. He was famous for a novel spiritual concept of art. Not painting in a realistic manner, he may be said to be the first expressionist, as early as 300 years before the advent of the style.

EPHEMERA   Small printed matter such as book plates, little signs, etc., designed and printed by printers for their own use and for their friends.

FAÏENCE   (French) Glazed, multi-colored pottery, named for the Italian town of Faenza, where much of such pottery was made.

FANEUIL HALL   An historic landmark in Boston, Massachusetts.

FESTSPIELE   (German, "festival plays" or "concerts.") Popular attractions for the cultivated tourist.

FINE ARTS MUSEUM   (Boston) One of the greatest museums in the United States. It maintains an excellent school of art at the college level.

FLACON   (French) Flask or small bottle.

FORMENTOR   A beautiful mountainous region of Mallorca, not far from the city of Palma de Mallorca. It has a splendid seaside hotel of the same name.

FRA ANGELICO   (Italian, "Brother Angelico;" *Fra* is short for the Italian *frate)* One of the most famous painters of the Renaissance, active in Florence, where he lived his life as a monk in a small, bare cell.

FRAKTUR   (Latin, "broken.") Lettering with a quill cut on a slant, producing strokes that can not be easily rounded, but seem broken when the direction of the stroke is changed.

FRANC   French and Swiss coin, roughly equivalent to an American quarter.

FRESCO   (Italian, "fresh") A method of painting in which specially prepared pigments are applied to a mixture of wet plaster and lime. The material is then allowed to·harden and become permanent. In this way both old and contemporary murals were created in public buildings. It is all but impossible to remove such works of art. During the flood in

Florence of 1966, many frescoes were partially or completely destroyed. Oil paints cannot be applied on plaster walls to achieve permanence. This fact accounts for the almost complete decay and fading of Leonardo da Vinci's "Last Supper." Perhaps he knew; perhaps not.

FUSILIER   (From French *fusil* for "rifle") Thus, a fusilier is a French infantryman.

GARE DE L'EST   The East Station, one of the five major railroad stations in Paris.

GAZPACHO   An Andalusian gastronomic specialty. A Spanish vegetable soup made by cooking one-half of a quantity of onions, tomatoes, green peppers and cucumbers. The soup is then chilled and the rest of the raw vegetables, finely minced, are added, but not cooked.

GEORGE III   The King of England who was unpopular with the American colonists. During his reign, some very fine furniture and beautiful silver were produced in England.

GETREIDEGASSE   (German "wheat lane.") The name of a small quaint street in Salzburg. The great Austrian composer, Wolfgang Amadeus Mozart, lived on that street with his family.

GEWURZTRAMINER   A famous Austrian white wine. *Gewurz* means spicy.

GONDOLA   The Venetian version of a slender canoe-like but steady boat used for transportation of people and goods. The gondolier stands elevated at the stern of the boat, propelling and steering it at once with one long oar, and shouting or singing a great deal of the time.

GOYA   Francisco Goya, a Spanish artist at the turn of the 18th Century, famous for both his paintings and etchings. His series of etchings *The Disasters of War* depict the cruel occupation of Spain by Napoleon's troops. During the last years of his life, Goya became insane but he still continued to produce fascinating works of art. Much of his work hangs in the Prado in Madrid.

GRABEN (German "The Ditch.") Part of the fortifications of medieval Vienna, outside the city walls. The Graben is now a popular street of fashionable shops.

GRANDE ARMÉE The great, magnificent army of Napoleon I, a conversation piece for the French ever since the "glorious" days of Napoleon.

GREENS PARK An attractive park in the center of London. It is near Hyde Park, Buckingham Palace, and Piccadilly.

GRENADIER A French artilleryman; specifically, one who handles grenades.

GRÜSS GOTT (German, "God greet thee.") A greeting used in Austria and sometimes in Southern Germany. The Swiss say *Griezi* which has the same meaning.

GUILDER A Dutch coin worth approximately 28 U.S. cents.

GUTENBERG, JOHANN Generally assumed to be the inventor of the art of printing. His home was in Mainz, Germany. Gutenberg printed the famous 42-line Bible, two columns of 42 lines of text per page, a very ambitious work at a time when only four pages could be impressed simultaneously with movable type. Preceding this Bible, Gutenberg printed the papal "indulgences," used to finance the building of St. Peter's Basilica in Rome. Gutenberg also printed the first missal.

HALBERD A combination lance and battle-axe. This weapon, popular in the Middle Ages, was decorative but unwieldy.

HARROD'S London's finest department store, located in the West End section near Kensington Park. It is famous for its magnificent flower and food departments.

HAYDN, JOSEF Great Austrian composer who preceded and outlived Mozart and who exercised a most important influence on the young musician. Haydn composed hundreds of symphonies, and a vast amount of other music.

HAYMARKET   A square near Covent Garden, London, probably the place where the early Londoners bought hay for their livestock and other supplies for themselves.

HAYSTACK   A pewter measure made in Ireland. It resembled an Irish haystack in shape.

HEIMATWERK   (German, literally, "work done in the homeland.") A governmental nonprofit institution, that encourages the peasants of the mountainous regions in Austria and Switzerland to produce artifacts such as wooden or pewter articles, woven and printed textiles, and many other products in the traditional manner of the region. These articles are made at home during the long winter months when the peasants are snowbound in the mountains, and have no way of making a living. The *heimatwerk* set-up makes it possible for the government to help its peasants without stigmatizing its citizens as the recipients of charity.

HOTEL ALFONSO XIII   One of the old great hotels of Spain. This charming building is situated in the center of Seville, midst all its street noises.

HOTEL LA F   A fictitious name for a hotel that is no more than a hovel. Absolutely international.

HOTEL SACHER   The great Viennese hotel, as charming today as when it was built in the 19th Century. It has probably the best cuisine in Austria, and is famous as the place which originated the *Sachertorte*. Located at the opera, the hotel is very convenient for both shopping and sightseeing.

HOTEL VIER JAHRESZEITEN   One of the two German hotels bearing the same name, which means "four seasons." One is located in Munich; the other, in Hamburg. Both hostelries are marked by a cultivated, restrained elegance that seems to be dying out. Both institutions offer the best cuisine and the best wines. However, they are each under different management.

HÜVÖS VÖLGY   (Hungarian, "cool valley.") A residential section of Budapest, which overlooks the city and the Danube.

HYDE PARK   One of London's old parks. Noted particularly for its famous Hyde Park Corner at Marble Arch where speakers of every ilk and persuasion, no matter how radical, may have their say, without interference by the law. Hyde Park, for the most part, resembles old meadows more than it does a cultivated garden. Traditionally, the gates are closed at nightfall.

ISLE DE LA CITÉ   A small island in Paris in the River Seine, bridged by the Pont Neuf (New Bridge). Notre Dame de Paris stands on this island.

INCUNABULA   (Latin "cradle prints.") All printed pieces done in the 50 years after the invention of printing in the mid-fifteenth century are called incunabula.

KAISER FRANZ JOSEF   Emperor of the Austro-Hungarian Empire for more than 60 years, the symbol of the friendly, easy-going atmosphere of Austria before the First World War. Nevertheless, he was a tragic figure. He lost his brother, Emperor Maximilian of Mexico who was executed by order of Benito Juarez in 1867; and his wife, Elizabeth who was assassinated by an anarchist in Geneva; his son, the Archduke Rudolph, who committed suicide at Mayerling; and then his nephew and heir apparent, the Archduke Franz Ferdinand, who was assassinated in Serajevo, Bosnia, in June of 1914. When World War I broke out soon thereafter, the 79-year-old monarch said, "Nothing is spared me."

KÄRTNERSTRASSE   Like the *Graben,* this is also a fashionable shopping street in Vienna.

KONDITOREI   (German, a confectioner's or pastry cook's shop.) A European institution. Even the smallest town is unthinkable without its little shop where fine pastries are made and served with coffee. In Austria, a *Konditorei* may be as famous as a hotel or a large restaurant, or the *Konditorei* may be simple in decor. Each *Konditorei* usually features its own specialties, never fewer than 20 to 30 varieties of excellent pastries. The atmosphere in such a place is leisurely; people often spend an hour or so sitting at little round, marble-topped tables, not very comfortably, but happily sipping coffee or hot chocolate and eating the delectable pastries.

KUNSTHALLE   (German, "hall of art.") An exhibition hall.

KURFÜRSTENDAMM   A residential thoroughfare in West Berlin, now becoming an elegant shopping district.

LACY   A term applied to some "Sandwich" glass because of the silvery, delicate appearance.

LAGO MAGGIORE   (Italian "The Major Lake") A large lake extending from Switzerland into Italy.

LAKE WINNIPESAUKEE   An American Indian name. This is the largest lake in New Hampshire.

LANDESKUNST MUSEUM   A museum housing representative primitive folk art—"The art of the land." Exhibits range from artifacts to reconstructed and fully decorated rooms of old farmhouses. The Landeskunst Museum in Innsbruck, Austria, has an extensive exhibit of Tyrolese art. Its counterpart in Munich, Germany, considerably larger in scope, is famous for its unique collection of "under-glass painting" and "votive" plaques, which are naive religious pleas or memorials.

LE SALON   The great Parisian automobile show, the first of its kind in the world. This annual fixture dates from the early 1900's.

LEFT BANK   The Left Bank of the River Seine, a section of Paris where students live and artists have their studios.

LIMATQUAI   An attractive street in Zurich, Switzerland, bordering the Limat canal and leading to Lake Zurich. It flows through the "Aldstadt," and is referred to in the oldest annals of the city.

LIMBURG   A small town in the Netherlands noted for its cheese.

LINGONBERRY   A Swedish variety of the American cranberry.

LITRE   One litre equals approximately one quart, or 1,000 cubic centimeters. All of Europe uses the metric system.

LOUVRE   Officially, "Musée du Louvre." It was originally built during the Renaissance by the French king, Francoise I, as his palace. During his lifetime, the art-loving king amassed and commissioned many fine paintings, among them the *Mona Lisa*. The beautiful statue, *the Venus of Milo*, as well as the famous *Winged Victory* dominate the major staircase in the museum.

MAJAS   The famed pair of oil paintings by Francisco de Goya in the Prado, Madrid which depict the Duchess of Alba, both dressed and undressed, in exactly the same pose.

MARIA SELBSTDRITT   A depiction of Mary with her mother Elizabeth and grandmother, Anna. All have halos. Religious pictures of this type were frequently painted under glass, and are sometimes mistaken for the Holy Trinity.

MARK   A German basic coin, roughly equivalent to twenty-five American cents.

MARZIPAN   A confection said to have originated in Persia. The origin of the word is too obscure to be explained satisfactorily. Marzipan is made of equal parts of grated blanched almonds and confectioner's sugar to which is added a small quantity of bitter almonds and some drops of rosewater. The best marzipan is made in Lübeck, Germany.

MAYFAIR   An elegant section of London which lies between Greens Park and Hyde Park.

MEMLING, HANS   One of the great Flemish painters of the Northern Renaissance.

MÉTRO   The subway of Paris.

METROPOLITAN MUSEUM OF ART   One of the finest museums of the Western World, this vast museum in New York City houses an unusual collection of Greek and Roman art, the arts of pre-Columbian South and Central America, a very fine collection of colonial furniture and silver (Paul Revere) as well as treasures of the Renaissance and of many other great periods of art.

MOUSSE AU CHOCOLAT   There are as many ways of preparing mousse au chocolat as there are inspired cooks. It is generally made of chocolate, eggs, brandy or rum, sugar, and cream. Additions and methods depend on the individual.

MOZART, WOLFGANG AMADEUS   The son of Leopold Mozart, a court musician in Salzburg, he is considered the greatest musical genius of the western world. Mozart became famous as a child prodigy, giving concerts at the age of six. He composed some 600 compositions in a short lifetime, dying at age thirty-four. These included six major operas, symphonies, many concerti, and sonatas for various instruments, and even short pieces such as the little song, "The Violet," based on the poem of the same name by Johann Wolfgang Goethe.

MURANO   One of several islands close to Venice, Italy, where the art of glass blowing has become internationally famous. The glass museum of Murano is well worth visiting. It affords a comprehensive survey of the history of glass, in a quiet, elegant palazzo, without the usual hustle and bustle of most museums.

NIPPES   A German term for knickknacks, such as figurines, seashell-encrusted picture frames, etc. During the Victorian era, nippes were a must for every household.

NORTHERN RENAISSANCE   It was inevitable that the Renaissance would make its influence felt throughout Europe. Northern artists such as the great German painter Albrecht Dürer went south to Italy to study under the Italian masters. When these artists returned, they influenced their own disciples and apprentices. The Renaissance then slowly made its way to Germany and to the northern part of France and Holland.

NOUVEAUX FRANC The "new" franc, France's revaluated currency, is worth about twenty American cents.

OPEN WINE Served in all localities where grapes are grown, open wine is kept in barrels. Often, it has not been fermented for very long. It is usually delicious and very inexpensive.

OPERNRING The major street of Vienna, so called because it ringed the city when Vienna was still walled, and because its most important building is the opera house.

PAELLA A national Spanish dish made of rice cooked with Saffron and additional ingredients such as chicken, shrimp, mussels, squid, etc.

PALACE OF THE DOGE In Italian, *Palazzo Ducale,* means "Palace of the Duke." The best-known Palace in Venice, it is situated on the Piazza San Marco, and is an eloquent masterpiece of Renaissance architecture. Constructed of white and pink marble, it is supported by massive, arcaded pillars. The second floor is supported by smaller, more delicate pillars. This Palace was the residence of the Doges, the rulers of Venice during the Renaissance.

PALAZZO (Italian, "Palace") Counterpart of "elegant mansion."

PALAZZO PITTI Famous Florentine museum of art.

PALMA DE MALLORCA The only sizable town on the island of Mallorca, itself the largest island of the Balleorics. This charming square-shaped island lies in the Mediterranean between Spain and Africa.

PARADA (Spanish, "bus stop.")

PATRON (French idiom, "the boss.") Generally, the owner of a small hotel or restaurant.

PENNSYLVANIA DUTCH   Misnomer for Pennsylvania Germans. This came about because the Swiss and the German emigrants who traveled down the Rhine River on rafts usually stopped in Holland, where they worked to earn their passage to America.

PESETA   A Spanish coin equivalent to one and a half cents in American money.

PEWTER   An alloy of tin and lead and sometimes copper. This metal has been popular since the Middle Ages in the manufacture of household articles. Pewter is easy to work and has a low melting point. In England, pewter is generally polished to a high gloss. In other countries on the Continent and in the United States, pewter is allowed to oxidize to an attractive dark gray color.

PHILADELPHIA MUSEUM OF ART   One of the finest museums in the United States, noteworthy for its comprehensive collection of Pennsylvania-Dutch folk art. The museum maintains a superior school of fine and graphic arts, including photography. College degrees are awarded to graduates.

PIAZZA SAN MARCO   The main and largest square in Venice, bordering the Canale Grande. On one side stands the Palazzo Ducale and the beautiful St. Mark's Cathedral with its Byzantine mosaics; opposite, looms the great Venetian library. The Piazza has numerous cafés and hotels and is always filled with tourists and pigeons.

PIESCHISSEL   A deep dish traditionally used by the Pennsylvania Dutch for baking pies. The common *Schissel* means bowl or deep dish. It is always decorated.

PIRANESI, GIOVANNI BATTISTA   Italian draughtsman of the 18th century, who was a great master of the art of etching. He had great admiration for classic architecture. His many and bold renderings of buildings and ruins stimulated a general interest in archaeology and in classical forms. Among his more unusual etchings are a group known as "The Prisons." These etchings are fantastically imaginative.

PLEYEL, IGNAZ   Austrian musician of the Haydn-Mozart period who emigrated to France and gained renown as a composer. The great concert hall in Paris is named for him.

PONTIL   The jagged mark made when a glass blower breaks the stem from the bottom of a bottle or glass which his assistant has been rotating. A pontil mark provides unquestioned proof that the glass was hand-blown.

PORRINGER   A vessel, sometimes made of pewter, with a delicate, flat, decorative handle. During colonial times, a porringer was used for feeding porridge to children.

PRADO   Spain's greatest museum. Although it is smaller than either the Louvre in Paris or the Metropolitan in New York, its paintings rank with the best in the world. The Prado has an extensive collection of Goya's paintings and etchings as well as Velázquez' and other great painters of the Renaissance and of the Baroque. The museum is within walking distance of Madrid's finest hotel, the Palace.

PRINZREGENTENSTRASSE   A street of elegant shops, restaurants, and theatres in Munich, Germany.

PRUNIER   A famous fish restaurant of quiet elegance, wide selection, and, reasonable prices, located in the center of Paris, not far from the Opera.

PUCCINI, GIACOMO   Italian composer of dramatic opera, of which *La Boheme*, *Tosca*, and *Madame Butterfly* are the best known.

PUTTI   Wooden and stone sculptures of cherub heads with wings, often used in quantity above the altar in a Baroque church.

PYTT-I-PANNA   (Swedish, "something in the pan") This is the name of a popular Swedish dish made of cubed steak, potatoes, and pickles all fried together, seasoned with a piquant sauce. Fried eggs are placed on top.

REFORMATION   The breaking away from Rome of several religious reformers independently seeking change in dogma and law of the Church of Rome. Martin Luther, a German monk, nailed his ninety-five theses on the door of the Castle church at Wittenberg on October 31, 1517. He sought, in particular, to fight the abuses and hypocrisies emanating from the papal chair down to the village parish. Eventually, the Reformation resulted in a confrontation between the fast-growing, powerful Protestant rulers of Scandinavia and eastern Germany and the loyal Catholic monarchs of western Germany, France, and Austria. This resulted in one of the cruelest wars of history, which decimated the European population and left in its wake (1618-1648) ruin, misery and the plague. During this holocaust, the iconoclasts or image-breakers ruined or stole enormous quantities of religious art from churches, monasteries, convents, and private homes. The plunder was particularly intense in Switzerland, and in England in the reign of Henry VIII.

REGENCY   See Biedermeier.

RENAISSANCE   (Literally, "rebirth.") A time in history when Western man had emerged from the Middle Ages and was ready to surge forward. Specifically, the term implies a rebirth of classicism in sculpture and architecture, a loosening from the stiffness of Byzantine painting, and the rise of new trends in philosophy and writing, theretofore rigidly controlled by the Church. But in a larger sense, the Renaissance man became involved with an appetite for new horizons. It was a time—the 15th and the 16th Centuries—that produced poets and philosophers such as Dante and Petrarch, painters such as Leonardo and Raphael, sculptors such as Michelangelo and Donatello. This period also produced Johann Gutenberg and his successors to make possible the dissemination of knowledge and beauty through the printing press. The dreams of Columbus and Magellan also came true, and scientists forged ahead in many fields. Ultimately, Martin Luther brought about the Reformation and translated the Bible into German. Mankind was impatient with the past, and ready for the future.

RIALTO   A famous covered bridge in Venice with shops on either side. It is mentioned by Shakespeare as the site of Shylock's business activities.

RIJKSMUSEUM One of the greatest museums of Western art in Amsterdam, the Netherlands. It is famous for Rembrandt's *Night Watch* and for Vermeer's small but exquisite *The Cook (Kuchenmeid)*. The museum possesses a tremendous collection of graphic art of the Baroque period, of artifacts of the Middle Ages, and an unusual collection of Japanese paintings, depicting the arrival and sojourn of the Dutch fleet in the harbor of Yokohama during the 18th Century.

SACHERTORTE A superior chocolate cake, first baked by Madame Sacher, proprietress of the Sacher Hotel in Vienna, but later claimed as their own by the famous *konditorei*, Dehmel, across the street from the hotel.

ST. GILGEN A small, attractive mountain village 20 miles east of Salzburg, situated at the lake of St. Wolfgangsee.

ST. GERMAIN Historic French suburb, the residence of King Henry IV and birthplace of the "Sun King," Louis XIV.

ST. WOLFGANGSEE (See St. Gilgen)

SALZBURGER KNOCKERLN There are as many versions of *Salzburger knockerln* as there are good cooks in Salzburg. Basically, this delicious dessert is made by beating whites and yolks of several eggs separately, with sugar, and baking them in the oven. The sugar in the mixture forms a light crust on this light and fluffy dish. Practically every Austrian restaurant will cook it for you to order.

SALZKAMMERGUT Literally, the "salt chamber." This section around Salzburg is so-called because of the salt mines which abound in that region. The section is also famed for its lovely mountain lakes and beautiful scenery, marred only by a good deal of rain.

SEINE The major river of France, originating on the eastern slope of the plateau of Langres, 18 miles northwest of Dijon. The Seine flows through Paris out to the Atlantic Ocean.

SIROP (Dutch, "syrup.") Made of molasses or fruit.

SLEEPERS Articles the values of which have been overlooked by auctioneers and public alike at auctions, but is discovered by one or more of the bidders.

SLIPWARE Decorated and glazed pottery, usually made in Pennsylvania or New Jersey during the 18th and 19th centuries.

SPANSCHACHTELCHEN (German, "split wood box.") Small to large, round and oval boxes made from finely split, pliable wood, usually decorated with colorful designs.

SPIEGELSTRAAT A street in Amsterdam, dotted with antique shops, close to the Amstelgracht and not far from the Rijksmuseum.

STEIN Called *Humpen* in German. A drinking vessel made of ceramic, pewter or glass popular through the ages and traditionally used for beer.

TAFELSPITZ One of the many Austrian versions of boiled beef.

TAUFSCHEINE (German, "Baptismal Certificate.") These were often hand drawn and lettered by primitive artists in Lancaster and Bucks counties in Pennsylvania. Later these were printed in the same primitive style by local printers, and then hand-colored. Still later, they were printed in three colors—usually red, yellow and black. Framed, they were used as decorative pieces in farm houses.

TEGELS (Dutch) Tiles.

TIENDA (Spanish) Small shop.

TINTERRIEN (Flemish) Pewter tureen.

TOSCANA The beautiful mountainous surroundings of Florence, Siena, and Assisi.

TRAUNSEE   A large mountain lake at Gmunden, Austria.

TYROLER   An inhabitant of Tyrol, an Austrian province, partly annexed by Italy in 1918, and now called Alto Adige.

UFFIZI   Great Florentine museum comparable to the Palazzo Pitti.

ULENSPIEGEL, TYL   (Till Eulenspiegel, literally "owls and mirrors.") A legendary figure of the Flemish section of the Lowlands which are sometimes called the "Protestant Provinces." Known for his practical jokes, Ulenspiegel has been immortalized by artists and writers, and by the composer Richard Strauss in his tone poem *The Merry Pranks of Tyl Ulenspiegel.*

UNCIAL   The first flowing writing form derived from the Roman alphabet. It was used by the scribes of the early Middle Ages.

UNGEFÄHR   (German, "approximately.")

UPSALA   An old Swedish university, of the same name as the town in which it is situated.

VAN DER WEYDEN, ROGIER   A Flemish painter of the Northern Renaissance; of the same era as van Eyck, David, Bosch, and others.

VAN DYCK, ANTHONY   Famous painter of the 17th century Baroque Flemish school.

VAPORETTI   Small Italian steamers capable of carrying 100 to 200 people for short hauls. They are used on the Lago Maggiore in the Swiss Canton Ticino and on the Canale Grande in Venice.

VELAZQUEZ, DIEGO   Famous Spanish painter of the Baroque period. He is particularly well represented in the Prado, Madrid.

VENINI   One of the finest Italian glass companies. It combines the best traditions of the past with the most modern technique and design.

VICTORIA AND ALBERT MUSEUM   This highly interesting museum contains a great display of English graphic art, Oriental collections, Regency furniture, and enormous tapestries woven by Renaissance weavers for the British court.

VIEJO   (Spanish, "old man.")

VILLA NEBRICH   A small "family pension" in St. Cilgen, Austria, accommodating about 30 to 40 guests. The presence of such pensions or villas is characteristic of European resorts.

VITRINE   A glass showcase used to display elegant articles, jewelry, antiques, etc.

VIVANDIÈRE   A camp follower and seller of food and drink, etc. They were extant from the Middle Ages to the mid-nineteenth century.

WALLOONS   French-speaking Catholics who inhabit Belgium, they stand in contrast to the Flemish-speaking Flamands. The Flamands are Protestants. Flemish is practically the same language as Dutch. These two groups are in opposition to each other.

WEGGLI   Traditional Swiss rolls.

WIESBADEN   A charming German spa near Frankfurt, untouched by World War II. For many years it was the headquarters of the American occupation forces. A number of American companies maintain their European offices in Wiesbaden. Wiesbaden has the characteristic elegance of the Central European spa, with its casinos and fashionable shops.

WINDSOR ROCKER   A style of English chair adapted by American colonists as a rocking chair.

WINTERTHUR (Switzerland)   A small town between Zurich and St. Gallen where the DuPont family originated. When they came to America and rose to fame and fortune, the DuPonts named their residence, and later on, the palatial museum they established after the little town in Switzerland.

WOLFESBORO A friendly new Hampshire town situated at Lake Winnipesaukee.

ZARZUELA A Spanish fish stew made of a variety of seafoods. The word *Zarzuela* is also used to describe a small traveling group of artists such as dancers, musicians, magicians, etc.

ZOUAVES Moroccans who served in the French army who wore their Moslem garb of voluminous pantaloons and open jackets. The Zouaves wore fezzes rather than caps or helmets.

The Index